"Lee Chin's life story, so eloquently and poignantly expressed, really resonated with me on a personal level. I could not put the book down until I finished the last page. This book is an inspiration to all who are passionate and determined to pursue their dreams in whatever career they may choose."

—**Carmee Lim, Mentor Principal of MindChamps Holdings, Founder and C-Edu-O of Aoede Music Enterprise Pte Ltd, and former Principal of Raffles Girls' School**

"This book, like Lee Chin herself, is bursting with life and energy! It combines tenderness and charm with tenacity and determination. People who see only the stellar violinist on stage or in the studio need to know something of the process by which she got there. In these pages you will read of someone who seized the day even though it meant leaving an environment of comfort and support, guided only by one question: 'How can I get better?'

Anyone with a desire to improve and advance will benefit from this book. It is not simply for elite musicians. Though we may know the principles in their dry and skeletal form – hard work, perseverance – this story puts flesh on these bones and brings them vividly to life. Lee Chin's story, written in such direct and accessible style, provides an almost palpable demonstration of the power of music to heal and triumph over adverse circumstances. In reading it, we get more than just an engaging story. It is like seeing the inner workings of a world-class performing artist.

Read it. Learn from it. Be inspired by it."

— **Peter Crookes, Professor of Surgery, Keck School of Medicine, University of Southern California**

Published by Straits Times Press Pte Ltd
Singapore Press Holdings
Mezzanine Floor, Information Resource Centre
Level 3, Podium Block
1000 Toa Payoh North, News Centre
Singapore 318994
Tel: (65) 6319 6319 Fax: (65) 6319 8258
stpressbooks@sph.com.sg
www.stpressbooks.com.sg

STRAITS TIMES PRESS

General Manager, Susan Long
Publishing Manager, Shova Loh
Business Development Manager, Juliet Lee
Creative Director, Lock Hong Liang
Editor, Eunice Quek PC

Printed in Singapore

**National Library Board, Singapore
Cataloguing-in-Publication Data**

Siow, Lee Chin, author.
From Clementi to Carnegie : the journey of Singaporean violinist Siow Lee Chin
/ Siow Lee Chin. – Singapore : Straits Times Press, [2015]
pages cm
ISBN : 978-981-4642-22-4 (paperback)

1. Siow, Lee Chin. 2. Violinists – Singapore – Biography. I. Title.
ML418
787.2092 -- dc23   OCN911260789

From *Clementi* *to* *Carnegie*

THE JOURNEY OF SINGAPOREAN
VIOLINIST SIOW LEE CHIN

SIOW LEE CHIN

Straits Times Press

CONTENTS

FOREWORD

I first heard about Lee Chin from my parents. A young violinist had been brought to their attention: still only a teenager, she had been offered a place to study at the renowned Curtis Institute in America and she needed sponsorship. Were they interested? Of course they were!

My father, Sir Percy McNeice, was always a great music lover. Every evening, the house would resound to the strains of the great orchestras of the world as he enjoyed his record collection, played at ever greater volume as he became progressively hard of hearing in his old age. My mother, Lady Yuen Peng McNeice, complained about the noise, but she loved music too, and she was also keenly interested in education, particularly the education of girls. Born to a Malaysian Chinese family in the early years of the twentieth century, she always regretted not having had the chance to go on to further studies herself, and she was determined to give that chance to as many young people as possible.

So began an acquaintance with Lee Chin that developed into a warm and delightful association with our family. My parents took great pleasure and pride in her progress, but they also came to love her as a person. And she amply repaid their affection, coming to see them whenever she was back in Singapore and playing, often with her brother Yew Nam, at family celebrations and, most touchingly, at the funerals of them both.

Lee Chin's story is a remarkable one. How many of us would have the courage and determination to travel to the other side of the world at such a young age, leaving behind home and family in pursuit of a dream? Lee Chin's account of her struggles and setbacks, her achievements and triumphs, makes for enthralling reading as she faces and overcomes the challenges of her new life. She shows us how to live life to the full, to seize the opportunities that come our way and to refuse to be daunted or discouraged. Through it all, she shows how music has the power to change lives and to transcend the boundaries of country and culture. While remaining a true Singaporean, she has become a citizen of the world and an inspiration to the students following in her footsteps.

My parents would be so proud.

Shelagh McNeice

Siow Lee Chin with Lady Yuen Peng McNeice on her 90th birthday

PREFACE

I have a habit of making New Year resolutions using the letters of the alphabet as a reference point. For the longest time, "B" stood for "BOOK".

Still, I had my doubts that anyone would be interested in reading about the life of a violinist from Singapore. To make matters worse, my dear brother Yew Nam, who has always kept me grounded with his frank advice, wasn't convinced that my book would fly off the shelves when I showed him my first drafts.

Without any real deadline to propel me forward, "B" remained unchecked on my to-do list. On one occasion, I was even told that I had used the word "dateline" instead of the intended word "deadline". Oh dear. I should be the last person to write a book!

So it came as a bit of a shock to me when out of the blue, a publisher invited me to tea, and suggested that I should consider writing my memoirs. They would be happy to publish it, they said. Great! But first, who could benefit from reading a book about me? And second, what should I write about?

As I pondered these two not unimportant questions, I realised that in numerous masterclasses I had conducted, I had encountered many students who aspired to pursue music, but didn't know how to convince their parents that this was a worthy profession. They always wanted to know: "How did you do it? What are my job prospects if I study music?"

It dawned on me that what made my young students and their parents sit up during my lectures and masterclasses, was when I shared how the lessons I learnt from music helped me in my own life. Performing music is so much more than just playing the notes. If I teach a student violin, I am teaching that person a way of life as well. While not everyone will become a concert artist, the lessons learnt from cultivating the discipline required to perfect your passion, mustering the patience to do the work before you taste success, and having the faith to persevere through setbacks, are valuable takeaways that will carry you through life.

I had left home at a young age to study music in America, and having to grow up without my family around me was one of the biggest sacrifices I had to make. Yet through it all, music was the bond that held my family and I together. Once, a friend of mine in the US asked me how I kept in touch with my family. I said I used a fax machine (a novelty for a student at that time). My friend misheard my reply, and responded incredulously, "You have a sex machine?!"

In anticipation of the inevitable question, I must preface that neither sex machines nor my love life are part of this story. This is a story of how my Singaporean upbringing and quirks helped me as I sought to share my love of music with people around the world. My journey has not been a bed of roses, but I count my blessings for family and friends who helped me along the way. Without their support, I would not be where I am today.

One person in particular was Lady Yuen Peng McNeice, who was like the grandmother I never had, and a wonderful inspiration and mentor.

The violin I am playing on today is a gift from her. When I asked how I could thank her, she said, "You should do something for another person. Use it to help others realise their dreams."

These words have inspired me to reach out and encourage young people to pursue their dreams, be it in music or otherwise. And as they say, where there's a will, there's a way. My travels led me to work with talented young people with a tremendous desire to learn. And in China, my eyes were opened to the amazing power of music to connect. In seeking to give back, I was embraced by kindness and generosity. When Mr Chan Ming Keng, Chairman of JingHope Holdings Pte Ltd, learnt about my story and this book, he pledged his wholehearted support. I am truly grateful.

Once again, I am reminded that if you can shed your fears and do what you love, the sky's the limit.

Siow Lee Chin

With JingHope Holdings Pte Ltd Chairman Chan Ming Keng and his son
Chan Yau Fei at my debut recital in Suzhou

WHERE I CAME FROM

When I was five, my dad, who was a violinist, thought it a good idea that I learn to play the piano. He soon discovered what a terribly uncoordinated child I was. On the keyboard, my left hand couldn't coordinate with my right. My fingers kept running away from me, like they didn't want anything to do with the rest of my body. My piano teacher, an unsympathetic and fierce individual, punished me severely, as if I were doing all this deliberately. Piano lessons were no fun at all, and I threw in the towel after only a few months.

Fortunately, that first obstacle in my musical education didn't set me back for too long. When Dad sat me down for my first violin lesson, my right and left hands, as if by magic, started behaving themselves.

Maybe I could have mastered the piano if I had stuck with it long enough. Then again, maybe it just wasn't meant to be. It's ironic, because most parents think the violin is a more challenging instrument than the piano for beginners. This may be true for many, but for me it was the reverse.

Several years after I had set my heart on becoming a concert violinist, I gained additional insights into what other professionals thought about this chosen instrument of mine. When I was doing my Artist Diploma at the Oberlin Conservatory in the United States, a brain surgeon approached my teacher Mr Vamos for violin lessons, claiming that playing etudes helped with his dexterity during surgery. Some time later, another surgeon told me that he found it more difficult playing the violin than performing an operation!

Even one of the most revered statesmen of our times, Singapore's founding Prime Minister, the late Mr Lee Kuan Yew, shared the same sentiment. In the wake of his passing in March 2015, many of his inspirational speeches resurfaced as the nation paid tribute to his visionary greatness and his ability to drill down to the core of issues. One of these was a speech he delivered at the inauguration of the Victoria Concert Hall in 1980. A hard-nosed realist who was never one to mince his words, he highlighted the challenges of identifying Singaporeans willing to make a career in music.

"The best musicians begin training from the age of three to five," he said. "It is a long and rigorous road, even for the gifted. Few gifted Singaporeans, with such good minds, ear and touch, will want to chance their careers in music. Any person with a mind capable of committing 120 20-minute pieces of music to memory, and a deft touch, can easily meet the demands of most traditional professionals; they can become surgeons, doctors, lawyers, or engineers, professions which provide a rewarding life, without continually disciplined efforts."

Oh dear! Had I known earlier, perhaps I would have chosen an easier profession, like pulling teeth!

Now that I also teach the violin, I encounter many like-minded pragmatic parents who want their children to reap the benefits of music, whether or not they eventually pursue it as a career. One of the most celebrated Nobel Prize winners of all time, Albert Einstein, was not only an outstanding scientist but also a passionate violinist. "Life without playing music is inconceivable for me," he declared.

His son, Hans Einstein, added of his father, "Whenever he felt that he had come to the end of the road or into a difficult situation in his work, he would take refuge in music, and that would usually resolve all his difficulties." [1]

Is there a correlation between music study and academic achievement? The venerable *New York Times (NYT)* highlighted evidence in the article "Is Music the Key to Success?"[2] that appears to support this. It seems more than sheer coincidence that many of the most brilliant minds from science to politics to media have attributed their professional success to musical training: America's founding father Thomas Jefferson (violin), former US president Bill Clinton (saxophone), political scientist and diplomat Condoleezza Rice (piano), film-maker Woody Allen (clarinet). According to the *NYT* contributor and former Deputy Managing Editor of the *Wall Street Journal*, Joanne Lipman, many high achievers "apply music's lessons of focus and discipline into new ways of thinking and communicating – even problem-solving."

Playing a piece of music involves the auditory, visual, motor and emotional centres of the brain. Brain scans reveal that there is more activity in the brain during a musical performance than there is during most other

19

---

1   Clark, Ronald W. (1971) *Einstein: The Life and Times*
2   Lipman, Joanne (2013) "Is Music the Key to Success?", *The New York Times*,
    http://www.nytimes.com/2013/10/13/opinion/sunday/is-music-the-key-to-success.html

activities. Children's brains show evidence of faster development when they are learning an instrument. Researchers are finding that music instruction not only improves children's communication skills, attention and memory, but may even close the academic gap between rich and poor students.[3] The phenomenal success of El Sistema, Venezuela's youth orchestra programme, has spurred similar social uplift projects across America and Europe. School and community-based music programmes enable social change by removing children from the snares of poverty, drugs and gangs, and developing their confidence, teamwork and creativity through participation in music classes.

I doubt my own Dad had any inkling of this when he gave me the gift of music. He didn't worry about whether I would be able to make a living or whether I would develop a better brain from playing the violin. He simply wanted to share with me something he loved dearly.

Dad (Siow Hee Shun) was born in Johor, Malaya, in 1935. He met and married Mom (Choong Siew Kum) in Kuala Lumpur.

Dad was the odd one out in his family. His brothers were industrious Hakka merchants – sons a Chinese family could be proud of. He, however, was a sensitive soul tuned to the beauty of the world around him, especially classical music. The radio brought him the sound of music, and so mesmerised was he by the voice of the violin that he started saving to buy

---

3   Kase, Lori Miller (2013) "Using Music to Close the Academic Gap", *The Atlantic*,
    http://www.theatlantic.com/health/archive/2013/10/using-music-to-close-the-academic-gap/280362/

an instrument for himself. Even more remarkably, he taught himself how to play it, until he had set aside enough money for lessons.

This wasn't exactly common for a boy growing up in the 1940s. For one thing, he suffered greatly during the Japanese Occupation. As a child, he had been bayoneted by Japanese soldiers and left for dead. Fortunately, God chose to save him, and he picked himself up and found his way to safety. The physical and emotional scars, however, stayed with him for the rest of his life.

As a child, I had seen the scars on his back and stomach, but only realised much later what they meant. My heart broke when I tried to imagine the terrifying ordeal he suffered. To his credit, he never once uttered a word against the Japanese. The only time I got a glimpse of how long the trauma haunted him was in 2003, when I was invited to perform with the Singapore Symphony Orchestra as the soloist in its debut tour of Japan. I asked Dad to come along with me but he declined. That was the only time he turned down an invitation to hear me play. How deeply the pain ran! He just could not bear to visit Japan, not even 58 years after the end of the Japanese Occupation. Despite the horrors of war, Dad never begrudged the younger generation. He was always gentle and generous, devoted to teaching music and raising his family.

Dad was always modest about his own playing. He said that he had "farmer's hands" and not the delicate hands of a violinist. He was unhappy with the way he held his thumb (violinists obsess over such things). So to fix it, he would keep it bent with tape while he slept. I'm not sure if that ever helped him but it showed he would do almost anything to improve his playing. Violin music with a singing tone, seamless lines and soaring climaxes was what mattered to him most.

21

My parents

Like many Chinese couples, my parents were hoping their first child would be a boy. When I arrived instead, they chose the Chinese characters for "beauty" and "gentleman" as my name, hoping that I would take on the honourable qualities of a gentleman along with the obvious benefits of being beautiful. I like to think that I have the best of both worlds.

True to form, Dad was happy for me to dress nicely and act all dainty, but he often told me that even as a girl, I could do anything a boy could. (I believe that children are very malleable, and when an adult tells and shows them things, these become true for them.) He gave me great confidence even before I became a violinist. I never doubted that I could achieve whatever I set my mind to.

Of course I didn't know it at the time but Dad bought me a violin when I was just three months old. I'm sure he was bursting with excitement when he bought it, but he kept his own feelings in check. While I was growing up, he never asked me to play it, even though it's what he had wanted more than anything else. His style was much more subtle. At that time, he had formed a small string ensemble, which he coached regularly. Several of its members later became professional musicians with the Singapore Symphony Orchestra (SSO) and the T'ang Quartet. Knowing how competitive I was, he slyly took me along on his coaching sessions to let me see how much fun everyone else was having. Once I saw all that fun, I immediately wanted in on the action myself.

Under Dad's guidance, I took part in my first competition at age eight. The boy before me had played a very flashy piano piece and I was sure he was going to win. I chose the lyrical *Méditation* from *Thaïs* by Massenet. Before I performed, Dad told me, "Don't compare, just do your best. Enjoy it and make beautiful music". That's exactly what I did, and to my surprise, I won! From that time on, I have always loved lyrical pieces.

I learnt very early on that I could always trust Dad's musical advice. He taught me that the loudest and flashiest piece wasn't always the best, and to look for beauty in the mundane. With a flashy piece, all you might think about is playing the notes. A lyrical piece, however, teaches patience – an essential virtue in life. This is a lesson I never forgot. Later on, when I went to the US for further studies, my professors taught me the same things that Dad cared so much about, especially in communicating the beauty of a musical phrase.

Dad became one of the SSO's pioneer violinists, and I, too, climbed on board as its youngest trainee member. Playing with a symphony orchestra when you're 11 or 12 isn't unheard of, but it isn't common either. The orchestra chairs were made for adults – my toes could barely touch the ground when I sat on them. I would spend my mornings at orchestra rehearsals with Dad and his colleagues before going off to school. After concerts, I tagged along with Dad and his friends for supper at Newton Circus hawker centre, where Dad would treat me to char kway teow[4] as a reward for being good.

While my childhood was unusual in these respects, in all other ways it was completely normal. We would do regular family stuff like playing games at home (Scrabble and Monopoly were our favourites) or going to the movies. Now that we have the Internet, we can watch whatever we want at any time, but back then, going to the cinema was a big event. We would all pile in the car and head to the Capitol Theatre or the cinema at Cathay Building. James Bond movies, in particular, were our family's favourite. The adrenalin started right from the opening scenes! I've always associated James Bond with exciting family excursions.

Our own family dramas were weaved into the action as well. One of Dad's quirks was that he liked to arrive for the show exactly on time, not a minute early or a minute late. He wanted to be walking into the theatre just as the lights were going down. Mom, on the other hand, was of the type who liked to get there early, so there was always a bit of tension. Given that the first few minutes of a James Bond movie were always a fantastic action scene, you didn't want to miss it. It was a close-call sometimes, but we always got to see the whole thing.

24

---

4   Stir-fried noodles which I still indulge in whenever I'm home!

Like all kids (there was just no way out of it), I attended school, first at Anthony Road Girls' School, before moving on to secondary education at Raffles Girls' School (RGS). Several of my best friends from primary school went with me to RGS. I wasn't very athletic, both by nature and by upbringing (my parents didn't want me to hurt my hands), so I was hopeless at team sports and had terrible ball sense. My awkwardness on the playing field was compounded by my fair complexion. Whenever I wore my PE (physical education) attire, I stood out with my embarrassingly white thighs. There was a running joke that if anyone wanted to look for Lee Chin, they just had to look for the whitest pair of legs, and there I would be.

I made up for my lack of athletic skills by being the representative every time there was a school concert. On cultural nights, I was always singled out to perform. I was happy to oblige, and it gave me confidence to know that there was something I was good at.

RGS is affiliated with Raffles Institution (RI) – an all-boys school – although both schools are not located on the same campus. I remember often riding the public bus to school, admiring the RI boys in their crisp white uniforms. Once, I sneaked off to a little party with some friends. Dad and Mom thought it was an all-girls party, but as parents always seem to do, they found out RI boys were going to be there too, and I was duly grounded. From then on, I realised I was never going to be any good at telling lies.

At home, Mom was "Chief-of-Staff" who kept everyone's schedules in order, including Dad's violin lessons. We marvelled how she could remember all the phone numbers of Dad's students without writing anything down.

25

Celebrating my birthday at home

Like a Dynamo battery, Mom was (and still is) full of energy! She took care of us all and everything in our little flat, first in Stirling Road and later in Clementi.[5]

One day, and for reasons best known only to her, she painted the entire flat shocking pink! When Dad came home, he thought he had entered the wrong house and was about to walk away when we shouted, "We're here! We're here!" Mom's such a spontaneous person. Painting a whole apartment on her own was all in a day's work.

---

5   To non-Singaporeans: Clementi is a suburban residential town in Singapore, named after the British colonial Governor of the Straits Settlements Sir Cecil Clementi Smith. Coincidentally, Clementi is also the name of a composer. Perhaps I was fated to be a musician!

Mom could whip up meals at lightning speed too. Every single day, we ate what seemed like a banquet. Dumplings, steamed fish, chilli crab, curry chicken, and mai-fun could appear on the kitchen table on any day of the week. She could walk into a kitchen and create a meal from what seemed like nothing. Mom used to complain half in jest that she never got a day off from cooking. Dad loved Mom's cooking more than anything we could find in restaurants. Why would he go anywhere else?

Although Dad was from the Hakka dialect group, my brothers Yew Nam, Yew Mun and I grew up speaking Mandarin and Cantonese with Mom and Dad. We learnt English at school, and thanks to my good friend Karen Tan's father, who was a wonderful English teacher, I picked up my love for reading. Karen played the violin, and was a member of the ensemble Dad coached. Instead of letting me idle away my time when I waited for Dad to finish his coaching sessions, Uncle Tan would take me to the second-hand bookstore nearby where I could lap up my weekly fix of Enid Blyton and Hardy Boys adventures. I couldn't get enough of them. The stories fed my imagination of a life beyond tiny Singapore, and I started to yearn for my share of adventures too.

One day, Uncle Tan introduced me to something a bit weightier: *The Diary of Anne Frank*. Although I was in primary school then, it dawned on me that one could still have big dreams despite spending years hiding in a closet. In the face of war, Anne Frank found her voice in writing, and had the courage to declare, "I want to go on living even after my death!" Her lofty ideals widened my eyes to the world beyond our little flat.

When I was about 15, the famous American violinist Aaron Rosand appeared as guest soloist with the Singapore Symphony Orchestra to perform Saint-Saëns' third violin concerto. There is a portion of this piece that's played in harmonics (high ethereal notes performed with a special technique), which left me in awe. It was magical, like heavenly bells, and it transported me to a different place.

Dad always encouraged me to play for visiting artists, and as it happened, Mr Rosand asked me to play for him. I didn't know it at the time but he was recruiting for Curtis Institute of Music in the US, one of the most renowned conservatories in the world, which counts conductor Leonard Bernstein, composer Samuel Barber and more recently, pianist Lang Lang among its alumni.

I asked Mr Rosand if I could warm up first and he said, "Sure, go ahead."

Instead of warming up with a scale as most would, I was so nervous I started playing the Sauret cadenza[6] from Paganini concerto #1 in D major. It was the piece I was learning then. Once I got started, I couldn't stop.

Mr Rosand was gracious and funny about it. He asked, "If you're going to warm up with that, what are you going to play next?"

It could have been disastrous.

Instead, he said, "Would you like to study with me at Curtis?" I was shocked. Right there on the spot, he offered me a place to study in America. I had always wanted to see the world but this was beyond my wildest dreams.

6 A cadenza is a technically challenging passage that showcases a soloist's virtuosity and flair.

Encouraged, I also made an audition recording for The Juilliard School in New York. Toy pianist[7] Margaret Leng-Tan, who was born in Singapore and was the first woman to earn a doctorate from Juilliard, took it to the famous pedagogue Ms Dorothy DeLay, who mentored generations of noted violinists, including Midori, Cho-Liang Lin and Gil Shaham. One day, while my entire family was at home, there came a phone call from China. These days, we're used to instant communication, but it wasn't all that long ago when an international call was a big deal. Ms DeLay had heard my tape and was personally calling to offer me a place in her class at Juilliard.

In a very short time, I had received offers from two of the top conservatories in America that are consistently ranked among the world's best. Now we had a decision to make. Dad had no hesitation – he was supportive of me going abroad. He once had the opportunity to study music in England, but he gave that up to settle down and start a family. He didn't want me to miss this once-in-a-lifetime opportunity. Mom was less enthusiastic because she was worried how I would cope being on my own. Eventually, she relented, and it was decided that I would go to Curtis.

In spite of the benefit of a full scholarship, there were still some financial hurdles to overcome. Curtis had no dorms, and living expenses in the US were substantial. Serendipitous help arrived in the form of Pastor Roy Yin of Saint Andrew's Cathedral, Singapore. Pastor Yin was godfather to one of Dad's students and was also acquainted with Sir Percy McNeice – the first President of Singapore's City Council – and his wife Lady Yuen

29

---

7   Yes, she really does play tiny little toy pianos. She's made a career of it and it's as wacky and wonderful as it sounds. Look her up online – you'll be amazed.

Peng McNeice. Lady McNeice was known for her philanthropic work. She oversaw the Loke Cheng-Kim Foundation (named in honour of her mother), which offered scholarships to young people. Pastor Yin told the McNeices about me and we arranged to meet.

To my joy, the Foundation's board not only agreed to sponsor my travel and living expenses at Curtis, they also wanted to meet my family and see where we lived. So one night, we had them all over for dinner. Mom, as you can imagine, was frantic, cooking all day and fussing over every detail. At the appointed hour, this group of very distinguished and very wealthy people arrived at our modest HDB[8] flat in Clementi. We were all very nervous, but we shouldn't have been. Our guests were most warm and gracious, and the evening was a great success.

Life has a way of bringing people together, and my family's meeting with Lady McNeice was one of those fortuitous moments that changed my life. She didn't just help students financially, she had a keen interest to know them personally and be involved with their lives. Over the years, she became like a grandmother to me. Even when she was in her 90s, she continued to be an active member of the community, attending concerts, sharing with me her love for gardening and photography, supporting environmental conservation, and inspiring others with her generosity and kindness.

I am truly blessed that from a young age, people like Lady McNeice took the time to get to know me, and to offer their help and encouragement.

8   To non-Singaporeans: The Housing Development Board (HDB) transformed Singapore from third world to first, and runs one of the most successful public housing programmes in the world. HDB flats are home to over 80% of Singapore's resident population. With about 90% of these resident households owning HDB flats, it is one of Singapore's proudest achievements.

She told me that it was important for me to experience different cultures in order to grow and mature as a musician. Having her support was a huge boost. It gave me confidence, and this sense of assurance would help me pull through many tough moments in the years ahead.

Armed with Dad's words of encouragement and Lady McNeice's blessings, I set off with my violin to study with Aaron Rosand in America. It never crossed my mind that music may not be the best way to make a living in pragmatic Singapore. I was an idealistic teenager, excited to see the world, with the will to make something of my life.

EXCUSE ME, HOW DO I GET TO CARNEGIE HALL?

So there I was, fresh off the boat from Singapore, standing at the doorway of the Curtis Institute of Music on Locust Street, Philadelphia, in my trainers and jeans, muffled against the cold in thick overcoat, pondering how many great musicians had been here before me, had crossed this very threshold. It was an awe-inspiring moment, and I felt more than a little heady. My reverie didn't last long and I was brought down to earth with a jolt when I realised a far more imminent problem confronted me. Students were expected to make their own arrangements for accommodation, and here I was, without any family or friends in the US that I could rely on. Before I could begin to learn the secret of how to get to Carnegie Hall, I first had to ask a more prosaic question: Excuse me, where do I stay?

As luck would have it, one of the first people I ran into along the hallways at Curtis was Beatrice Long, a talented Taiwanese pianist who was also studying there. We hit it off at once and have been the best of friends ever since. Although going to college at 15 or 16 may seem a tad young to many, there were students even younger than me at Curtis, which does not have a minimum age for admission. Some were as young as 11 or 12 – they made me feel old! I naturally gravitated towards the older

Fresh off the boat at Curtis

students, for they seemed worldlier by comparison. Beatrice, who was all of 18, volunteered to share her apartment with me, and before long had assumed the mantle of my guardian. Once my parents knew of this, they breathed a sigh of relief for a huge weight was lifted off their minds.

I moved into Beatrice's studio apartment, and later, we moved to a slightly larger place. Both apartments had one thing in common: they were cold. To save on utilities, we were frugal with the heater, so frugal in fact that most of the time we would wear three pairs of socks, and at night sleep under as many blankets as we could beg, borrow, or steal.

In the midst of my first year at Curtis, I was blessed with two wonderful surprises, which came around the same time as my birthday.

First, I experienced snowfall, and second, I received news that led to my debut performance in America. And it wasn't to be in the school's recital hall, but at Carnegie Hall!

And so it was, one freezing day in February, that I found myself headed along New York's Seventh Avenue for one of the most prestigious music venues in the world: the place where Sinatra had crooned, where Pavarotti had cried, and where Justin Bieber had... whatever it was that he did. Actually, truth be told, the whole Curtis Symphony Orchestra was headed for Carnegie Hall with the same purpose as I.

I just tried not to think about it.

The school was in a state of excitement at the prospect, and it was not just because of the history of the magnificent building and what it stood for, but more so because the legendary 72-year-old Romanian maestro Sergiu Celibidache, who as a young conductor had led the Berlin Philharmonic, was making his North American conducting debut there. And he was making it not with a professional orchestra, but with us – the Curtis Symphony Orchestra! The only fly in the ointment, which kept the more mentally frail of us up at nights, was of his well-publicised arrogance and of his biting and controversial comments about his colleagues and fellow musicians. I once read one of his quips in *The New York Times*, which made me chortle over my Singaporean soft-boiled egg breakfast, but did little for my nerves. While being interviewed, the interviewer had remarked that Herbert von Karajan was famous. To which Celibidache had responded, "So is Coca-Cola." It seemed like he could get away with murder, and maybe he had. It was something I tried not to dwell on.

He demanded four or five times more rehearsals than anyone else had ever demanded. Which professional orchestra could afford 18 rehearsals

34

before a concert? Only a student orchestra could meet his terms, and Curtis convinced him to make his American debut for a benefit concert to celebrate the Institute's 60th anniversary.

As a young student orchestra, we had no idea what to expect other than he was going to be impossible to work with, surely. In person, everything about him appeared larger than life: from his towering and imposing stature to his full head of snow-white hair. He was the archetypal maestro straight out of a movie set. And such charisma! Very much like a hypnotist's. Sitting in the orchestra under his direction, you couldn't fail to be mesmerised. He could command you with just one icy look.

We worked hard, and contrary to his forbidding reputation, he was kind and personable, and was a fine and demanding teacher. Once, during a rehearsal, he explained why he was so demanding.

"If you have very little potential," he said in thickly accented English, "no matter how much you practise, it doesn't matter. The better you are, the more you need to practise. If you have a lot of talent, all the more you need to practise."

My young and impressionable mind soaked up these words to the extent that I, too, have become a perfectionist, at times driving my own students up the wall. When they don't practise, I do a Celibidache: *Talent is like a diamond. You need to polish it to see the brilliance. Do you want to be a rock or a diamond?*

I digress. Back to Celibidache.

He was a taskmaster on the podium, his attention to detail was painstakingly meticulous. He made us feel like we were going on a journey with him, something akin to the musical equivalent of climbing Mount Everest. I had never felt more prepared for a concert, and every one of us

35

was bursting with anticipation. The piece that sticks in my mind most is Wagner's Prelude and Liebestod from *Tristan und Isolde*. *Tristan* has the distinction of being considered the most erotic musical work ever written, and the unresolved cadence, which seems to go on forever, is like the music world's equivalent of an extremely long orgasm.

During one dress rehearsal, as the music was building to its climax, the orchestra got so caught up in the raw passion that, one by one, the musicians started to cry. We were collectively enveloped in this spiralling orgasmic outpour. It was an intoxicating combination for an orchestra of hormonally driven youngsters led by the cult figure of a 72-year-old, white-haired maestro.

Off-stage, Celibidache was surprisingly approachable. Once, a fellow student threw a party, and guess who appeared? We were all pleasantly surprised to see our most revered maestro let his hair down and boogie. This legend, who didn't care two hoots for music managements and public opinion, won our hearts simply by hanging out with us.

When concert day finally arrived, we were all charged up. I may be wrong, but I seem to remember being told that the line-up at Carnegie Hall that week included four of America's top A-list orchestras and *us*! Playing in that concert was like a dream for me. The audience consisted of many of America's top movers and shakers, and they certainly moved and shook to us. I had never before experienced non-stop applause and round after round of curtain calls. At some point, people started clapping in unison and stamping their feet, refusing to let us go.

The mood was electrifying!

It was one of those rare magical moments that I am so grateful to be a part of. It may be uncool to go against the grain, but Celibidache didn't care. He went after his vision of music par excellence. Stage performances look effortless because you're supposed to have worked out all the kinks when you practise.

When we finally left Carnegie Hall for our bus back to Curtis (we were students after all, and I had to wait a few more years before I had my first taste of limousine service), we were mobbed like rock stars. The next day, *The New York Times* published a glowing review, which elevated the status of this concert to the stuff of legends.

Many of my Curtis friends who were part of that concert have gone on to distinguished careers: Los Angeles Philharmonic concertmaster Martin Chalifour, Grammy Award-winning producer and engineer Da-Hong Seetoo, Miami String Quartet's former first violinist Ivan Chan... I could go on. To this day, whenever we manage to catch up, we can't stop talking about what a great concert that was. What an awesome ride.

For me, it was an early lesson from a maestro: Hold yourself to the highest standards. It was life-changing to see someone in his 70s still striving for perfection. These days, things are expected to happen fast, students too, expect instant results! I am often asked, "What does it take to be in your position? How many hours of practice does it take?" Celibidache taught me, and I now tell my students: There are no shortcuts; never have been, never will be.

That old chestnut of yesteryear still holds true – *Excuse me, how do I get to Carnegie Hall?* The answer: *Practise. Practise. Practise.*

And practise I certainly did.

Every student at Curtis could reasonably assume that they were the best musicians their hometowns and countries had to offer, so there was plenty of inspiration (as well as competition). All schools have rules, and

37

like most students, we broke them when we thought we could get away with it. For instance, the practice rooms closed at 11 pm. There was a big burly guard with a deep booming voice called Clarence who would come round to make sure the rooms were empty, and when satisfied that they were, would lock the doors. Our idea of being rebels was to stay in the building after hours and practise as long as we could. Such hellions!

The problem was that once we had finished, we couldn't leave by the normal exits, so we had to sneak out of the windows via the fire escape. Looking back, it was hardly the height of rebelliousness, but at the time, it seemed like we were players in a Nancy Drew mystery.

There were times when I felt like I was living out some of the stories I had read in books. Coming from a young country, Curtis was a completely different world than I had ever experienced in Singapore. It was steeped in tradition. Every Wednesday at 3 pm, we would have afternoon tea with Mrs Bok (her late mother-in-law Mary Louise Curtis Bok Zimbalist had founded and gifted Curtis with a generous endowment in 1924) and a special guest. There would be a big Russian *samovar* in the middle of the table, and we would have to dress nicely and make small talk with one another. This weekly event was part of our training as musicians. It wasn't just about drinking tea; it was about learning and practicing our social skills. They wanted us to be able to relate to our audiences, and learn the important art of communication.

I had regular lessons with my teacher Aaron Rosand. These were somewhat formal as well – no shorts and flip-flops. The teaching studios were housed in a former mansion, and a rather grand one at that. There were elegant antiques, ornate paintings and rich Oriental rugs. Rosand loved his cigars, and after my lesson, besides his insights, the smell of his cigars would always linger on. A world-class virtuoso, he exuded elegance in his musicianship. I was privileged to hear his playing up close and personal whenever he taught me. His signature glissando[9] emulated the expressiveness of the human voice. Just hearing the beauty and timbre of his sound taught me so much.

Rosand's primary teachers had been Leon Sametini and Efrem Zimbalist, who in turn were disciples of Eugène Ysaÿe, the King of the Violin, and Leopold Auer, a Hungarian violinist who had studied with Joseph Joachim. Regarded as one of the most significant violinists of the 19th century, Joachim was a close collaborator of Johannes Brahms and protégé of Felix Mendelssohn, both musical giants of the 19th century. Rosand had a rather formal style of teaching and he taught with such a distinguished air that I always felt in awe whenever I played for him.

I also took lessons from Jascha Brodsky, who was in his 70s at the time. He had been at Curtis for many years and had become something of a legend. Brodsky had played for the Russian composer Sergei Prokofiev, performed with pianist Vladimir Horowitz and studied with Ysaÿe. Years later, when it became popular to trace one's genealogy, it dawned on me that through Rosand and Brodsky, I could trace my own musical lineage to Joachim and Ysaÿe, and in turn, Ysaÿe's teachers Henri Vieuxtemps and Henryk Wieniawski – composers who are still very much played today. What an honour to be part of this rich musical tradition!

Like Rosand, Mr Brodsky liked to smoke. He would usually have a cigarette in hand when he taught, and sometimes even when he played (he

39

---

9   A glide from one pitch to another, performed by sliding one or more fingers over the strings of the violin.

Jascha Brodsky

would hold the cigarette in his bow hand)! He was always approachable and interested in getting to know his students not just as musicians but also as people. He always took the time to get to know each and every one of us. Occasionally, he would take me out to a nice restaurant, something I didn't do very often on my student's budget. He had the gift of making me feel important, like what I was doing actually mattered. I was very touched and it became a memory that I have always held on to.

Mr Brodsky was a big fan of violinist Oscar Shumsky. He gave me some of his LPs, which I still have up until this day. He would make me listen to them with my eyes closed so I had to concentrate on the music and nothing else. Later, he became my main teacher at Curtis when Mr Rosand began travelling frequently.

Another wonderful Curtis tradition was that whoever was conducting the Philadelphia Orchestra that week would conduct the Curtis Symphony Orchestra on Saturday mornings. With the Philadelphia Orchestra ranked among America's top orchestras, we had the benefit of being trained by some legendary maestros. For me, the most memorable were Leonard Bernstein and Riccardo Muti.

Bernstein would come dressed in a tracksuit with a towel around his neck – he literally ran to the podium! Without saying a word, he would just start conducting – and what magic he wielded with his baton! He conducted as if he were dancing. He was so relaxed, and way too cool for us kids.

Riccardo Muti, then the Music Director of the Philadelphia Orchestra, rarely came to conduct. One Saturday morning before orchestra rehearsal, however, I was in the girls' bathroom when suddenly a whole herd of girls stampeded in to check their appearances in the mirror. *What the heck was going on?* I wondered. When I went for rehearsal, I understood what the commotion was all about: Riccardo Muti was conducting this morning! On the podium, his power to mesmerise became even more apparent. Riccardo Muti had that chiselled dark and brooding Italian don look that was accentuated by his musical brilliance. We (especially the girls) were entranced by the magical power that seemed to flow from his baton.

In today's terms, he was *simply hot.*

New York solo debut at Carnegie Weill Recital Hall

Soon after I graduated from Curtis, I secured another gig at Carnegie Hall. This time, it was my New York solo debut in Carnegie Hall's 1991 Centennial Season. For any young artist, this is a big deal. However, getting a concert date at Carnegie is just the first step. How to fill the hall is a far bigger challenge.

I had just won the Artists International Young Artist Competition, but I was not delusional. Although the Weill Recital Hall is the smallest of the three stages at Carnegie ("intimate" being the politically correct word), finding 268 people to listen to a relative unknown on any night in

New York was going to be harder than the Schoenberg Phantasy[10] that my teacher Felix Galimir made me play from memory. Plus, I had competition. That week, Yo-Yo Ma was also playing in New York.

The concert promo poster did nothing to make me look like the sexiest star in town. I needed a photograph for the poster and I could only afford a couple of hundred dollars. These were the days before I had stylists. The result was an au naturel portrait that made me look like the girl next door from Clementi. What was I to do?

Out of the blue, I recalled a story Dad once told me about the violinist Henryk Szeryng who had both Polish and Mexican citizenship. Whenever he gave a concert, he would call the embassies of both countries. Each embassy would send a limousine to receive him and he would pick the fancier car and travel to the concert hall in style. To my naïve mind, the embassy seemed to be where I should get help.

I picked up the courage and paid a courtesy visit to Ambassador Chan Heng Chee, then Singapore's Permanent Representative to the United Nations. She was based in New York, so she seemed to be the right person to ask. The epitome of a successful diplomat, Ambassador Chan was impeccably dressed and oh-so-elegant. I was more than a little intimidated, but then I figured, what did I have to lose? I told Ambassador Chan about my recital.

"Can you help me?" I asked.

"Why should I help you?" she responded.

She had asked an important question. Why should anyone help me?

43

---

10 Arnold Schoenberg's Phantasy is a challenging piece that is not usually played from memory. Galimir made me do it because he said I needed to do something special in my New York debut.

I had to prove myself worthy. I thought quickly and replied that whenever I attended a concert by a Japanese artist, I would see many Japanese in the audience. Could Singapore do the same? Can we encourage Singaporeans who are living abroad to support their own artists?

It paid off because Ambassador Chan did help me. She made some phone calls. One thing led to another and before I knew it, Singapore Airlines agreed to promote my concert to their VVIPs. They invited their special guests and threw an open bar reception at the Russian Tea Room – the iconic New York restaurant across the street from Carnegie Hall, where legendary artists celebrated after their concerts. Thanks to Ambassador Chan and Singapore Airlines, the turnout at my recital was amazing! People I didn't know came to hear me play. It was pretty cool as far as New York debuts went.

I played a challenging programme that my teacher Felix Galimir recommended, including Beethoven's Sonata in D major, Prokofiev's Sonata in F minor (I learnt this work from Jascha Brodsky, who had performed with Prokofiev), and of course, the Schoenberg Phantasy from memory. On hindsight, it was the best advice anyone could have given me at that time. I was forced to learn an incredibly difficult programme, which helped me to win bigger competitions later on. I had no idea of the importance of this at the time, and of what was to follow. I just complained to Mr Galimir how hard it was to be a concert violinist.

"Well," he said, "by definition you're already a masochist by choosing to be in this profession: Musicians have to keep striving, and there's no guarantee you will make it."

Galimir was right. There are still no guarantees. One just has to go for it. Dream big. Do the best that you can and *go for it*.

AIR ON A SHOESTRING

When I moved to New York, I had the romantic notion that within a couple of weeks I would be playing to appreciative audiences, making powerful connections, selling millions of CDs; basically, taking New York by storm, heck, taking the whole world by storm! And then after the storm, move to Beverly Hills, marry Johnny Depp and live happily ever after.

Much to my chagrin, things did not turn out quite as planned. Oh well, you know what they say of the best laid plans of mice and men!

Between classes at the Mannes College of Music where I was doing my Masters, I was gritting my teeth playing Pachelbel's Canon at countless weddings (for some reason, they requested this all the time), fiddling in the orchestral pit in Broadway theatres, and generally subbing in any orchestra that needed a subbing fiddler. Living in New York was expensive and I was busy finding ways to make ends meet.

Broadway shows paid good money and many struggling musicians were on waiting lists for these gigs. I could make more than $1,000 per week playing in musicals. But musically, I felt under-nourished. Would I spend the rest of my life in a pit orchestra? In a pit of despair?

I did my share of orchestral auditions, and didn't get very far. Maybe my heart wasn't really in it. My ambition was to be a soloist. Playing in an orchestra required a completely different skill-set. As a young trainee filling in for the Singapore Symphony from the back of the violin section, I had seen the guest soloists in action. To be on stage with the orchestra behind you, making music together has to be one of the most thrilling experiences for a musician. To this day, it still gives me goosebumps just thinking of it.

But how do I get there? At the front of the stage? Under the spotlight? In a pretty dress and with a demure smile on my lips?

At this time, I had just won a small competition and was beginning to get a few concerts, but it was really challenging to get under the spotlight unless you were very well connected or had powerful management.

Although I was facing an uphill struggle in my ambitions, there were enough pluses to keep my enthusiasm kindled. I met many interesting people along the way who cared a great deal about music.

The late Jens Nygaard, especially, was very kind to me. He invited me to play in the Jupiter Symphony, which he formed for young people. I played occasionally as concertmaster. We performed in Alice Tully Hall at Lincoln Center, and did all the Mozart and the Beethoven symphonies – the classics. Nygaard had named the orchestra after the beautiful gaseous planet Jupiter. To him, it was a symbol of musical perfection: intangible, unattainable but worth the effort. Looking back, it seemed to reflect the state of my dream to be a soloist.

One time, Nygaard offered me a solo spot with the orchestra. I was invited to play the Mozart Adagio for Violin and Orchestra. As much as I loved Mozart, this was a little five-minute piece, and painfully slow-going.

I wondered how I could take New York by storm with this Adagio.

I was very nervous when I went on stage. In my heart, I decided to dedicate the piece to my friend Chris who was ill with a rare form of brain cancer. Strangely, this calmed me down. When I started to play, the nervousness disappeared. It was not about me anymore. Through the music, I was able to express my anxiety and concern for a friend who was going through a difficult time. It was very cathartic and moved the audience too. I was pleasantly surprised when I received a nice review.

Despite these memorable musical moments, I found time for a few distractions. I went to parties where there were people other than musicians. I loved to party and gallivant in SoHo. I also developed a taste for going to the movies, which in New York is an experience different from that in any other city. The audiences were – and still are – discerning and vocal, especially if the director or cast is one of their own. Whenever a new Woody Allen movie came out, everyone went to see it and everyone had something to say about it. The artistic energy was intoxicating. Another of my pastimes was to read *The New York Times* on Sunday (it still is) over a bagel with lox and cream cheese, and check out the reviews. It gave me a real kick to be at ground zero, the place where the action was.

Along with the animate, there was also the inanimate. I was surrounded by beautiful architecture, old and new. I loved the Guggenheim Museum and the iconic Plaza Hotel overlooking Central Park. My favourite place was the Museum of Modern Art. It's not so big that it's overwhelming and the art is top notch. Every week, there's a night when it's free for students, and that's when I would go there and peruse.

New York was also a food mecca. For a Singapore girl, this little detail was right up there with the parties, the movies and the Guggenheim. The city had such gastronomic variety! This was where I grew fond of Japanese food and I could often be found searching the back lanes for a good sushi bar. Then there was Chinatown, of course. My Chinese friends, including those who came to visit, would head for the place like iron filings to a magnet to gorge on dim sum.

As you have probably already gathered, I enjoyed New York tremendously.

One of the problems for a student in New York was finding a place to stay; it was almost as difficult as finding a job. When you rent a place in New York, you usually have to go through a plethora of security checks; picky landlords would ask for references. As I couldn't afford a fancy apartment, I had to put up in unsavoury places in some pretty tough neighbourhoods.

One day, I saw an advertisement in a shop window for a place on 71st Street off West End Avenue and went to check it out. Paul the landlord, who was an architect from Russia, together with his wife Anna from the Czech Republic, lived in a beautiful brownstone house. It was close to Lincoln Center and they had renovated the place and partitioned it into 10 apartments. The fancier ones were rented out to opera singers from the Metropolitan.

They interviewed me briefly, and I expected them to ask for the obligatory reference, like most landlords, so I was shocked when on the spot they agreed to rent me an apartment, with almost no questions asked. Well, no difficult questions anyway.

Don't you need a reference? I asked. They said no. It was then I realised that I must have been born with an honest face, and that clearly I didn't resemble a serial killer (although some of my current students might give you a good argument on that one).

It turned out, quite simply, that the couple loved the arts. Most of their friends were either singers or writers. They rented to people they liked, and they must have thought that I couldn't be so bad if I was a musician.

The apartment I rented was a work in progress. It was not completely renovated, but at least it was reasonably priced, and the whole place was tastefully and elegantly done up. The landlord had personally designed every nook and cranny himself. When I went away for the summer, they allowed me to store my things there for free. We became good friends. To this day, we still keep in touch.

I had a daily routine, which included many pit stops on my way to school. From my apartment on 71st Street to Mannes on 85th, I would walk along Broadway and stop at Zabar's for knish[11] and the best coffee in town. It was a New York institution and a favourite hangout for musicians. You never knew who you would run into there. Just a stone's throw from Zabar's was Citarella, the ultimate gourmet grocery. I always stopped by to gaze at the mouth-watering selection of fresh seafood. They had an amazing window display where a Mexican guy would use the catch of the day to form artistic designs. Every morning, I looked forward to seeing how he would come up with a different display. He was so creative and fish was his medium of expression.

Although Mannes did not have the Ivy League status of Yale, I declined a full scholarship from Yale (and Rutgers University) to do my Masters at Mannes because of Felix Galimir.

49

---

11 A snack popular in the Jewish community. Essentially, a curry puff without the curry.

Mr Galimir had taught me at Curtis. He was Jewish, and a giant of a musician despite his small stature. Short with bushy eyebrows, he spoke in a loud, sharp voice that was almost a shriek. Oh, what I would give to hear that shriek again! It was his hallmark. At heart, he was a kind and gentle man who cared a lot for his students. His love of music was infectious. He knew his stuff and if you were unprepared, you would hear no end of it. At Curtis, everyone was both awed and terrified by him. Yet, everyone wanted to study under him.

Curtis has a humbling tradition. In orchestra, new students have to pay their dues, being assigned seats at the back of the second violins. The more senior we became, the more upfront we moved. It was the same for chamber music. New violin students typically played second violin rather than the flashier first violin parts. I didn't know it at that time, but Mr Galimir always picked on the second violins because he believed the inner voices of the music were critical to a great performance. When he kept picking on me, I thought he didn't like me, so I was very surprised when he expressed interest to teach me after I graduated from Curtis.

At Mannes, I had lessons with him at least twice a week. He would sit in a chair in a corner of the room when he taught me, and if he didn't like the way I played, he would cringe, shrinking himself into the chair, making himself smaller and smaller. That was how physically he reacted to music. I felt so terrible for inflicting such pain on dear Mr Galimir that I would work extra hard.

Galimir had studied with the legendary Carl Flesch whose scale system is still the "Bible" for violinists. Galimir developed his own scale exercises that took two and a half hours from start to finish. He expected his students to practise these scales every day. One Saturday morning in

New York, I was awoken by the ringing of my phone. It was Mr Galimir. "Have you done all your scales yet?" was the first thing he asked. At eight in the morning, I didn't know whether to laugh or cry.

As a rule, violinists have to work out their own fingerings for each piece, and they don't give them out easily. Good fingerings are incredibly helpful. Sometimes, I came up with a certain fingering that didn't make sense.

"What kind of mashugana[12] fingering is that?" he would say in his Yiddish way. He'd then show me his way. "If you like it," he joked, "you will have to give me a quarter." His sense of humour was endearing, and just another part of his unique makeup.

These days, to impress my students, I will sometimes show them what Galimir taught me.

"These fingers are from Mr Galimir," I will say. "If you like them, you will have to give me a quarter." I get interesting responses. American students would be ready to challenge me for the quarter whereas my Chinese students would look duly impressed. Most parents of younger Chinese kids would sit through the entire lesson taking notes, fingers at the ready to reach into their pockets to hand me the quarter!

Mr Galimir had a fresh and colourful way of teaching. He loved using analogies to make his point. The lipstick analogy was one of his favourites.

"Do you wear lipstick when you go on a date to the opera?" he once asked me when commenting on my vibrato. I said yes. "What if you go to the beach? Do you wear the same lipstick then?"

51

12 A Jewish term for something crazy or bizarre.

He complained that my vibrato was beautiful but always the same. If things are predictable and beautiful all the time, it becomes mundane. The beauty is in the contrast.

"Your vibrato is your lipstick," he continued. "You cannot have the same lipstick for different occasions." That stuck in my mind.

When I found out, only recently, that Galimir loved collecting rare clocks, I got a deeper insight into what made this great musician tick (excuse the pun). As how all the intricate parts of a clock put together make a great timepiece, so he had a way of showing how all the different parts of the music came alive as one organic piece. After a coaching session with him, there was always clarity.

Clarity probably comes with age spots and wrinkles. When you're in your twenties, any kind of clarity is rare. Galamir sensed it. All great teachers have a way of touching you when you are in doubt. Once, he pulled me aside.

"I believe in you."

He was not one with flowery words. He cut to the core. These were exactly the words I needed to hear. It meant a lot to me. I pushed myself extra hard so I could live up to his expectations. When I graduated, Mannes threw in the Performance Award given by the college to its most outstanding graduating student.

Despite this, I still couldn't see where I was going with the little breaks I had so far. New York was exciting but I didn't feel especially fulfilled. I had serious doubts about how I was going to make ends meet if I wanted to be a soloist. Being a kiasu[13] Singaporean, I thought I should have a Plan B.

---

13 A Singlish word, which means "fear of losing".

I considered other career options.

I watched TV and loved listening to the radio. At the time, a radio show called *Dr Ruth* was all the rage. I was both intrigued and amused. Dr Ruth, an elderly Jewish lady who spoke English with a heavy German accent, was an unlikely star, doling out no-nonsense advice on life and sex and becoming a household name as a pop psychologist. She was entertaining and her advice made sense. I enjoyed listening to her, and it set me thinking. I have always been a people person, and I am fascinated by how the brain works. Perhaps I could be a psychologist and dispense wise words on music and life? However, when I investigated further, I found that I needed to get a doctorate degree and several years of internship before I could practise as a psychologist. It would take six to eight years! I was not prepared for this, so I decided, *What the heck, I'll stick with music.*

I had left home in my teens, and before I went Curtis, Dad had been my sole teacher. Instinctively, I gravitated towards teachers who cared for me. It was around this time that Aimee Kreston, my roommate at Curtis, told me about the Vamoses. Aimee was almost six-feet tall with flaming red hair, and I was this slightly vertically challenged (sans heels) Asian girl with black hair. We were the odd couple at Curtis but got on like a house on fire. She had taken violin lessons from Almita Vamos in Chicago, and she adored the Vamoses.

I heard how cool the Vamoses were from many others too. Another Curtis schoolmate, Sigrun Edvaldsdottir, now concertmaster at the Icelandic Symphony, had also studied with them. They had a cult-like following. Years later, Amy Chua would recount in her *New York Times* bestseller *Battle Hymn of the Tiger Mother* how she mobilised her entire family for an 18-hour drive to Mrs Vamos' studio in the hope that her daughter Lulu would be accepted as Mrs Vamos' student. Had Mrs Vamos actually agreed, Tiger Mom, who wanted nothing less than the best violin teacher for Lulu, admitted that she would readily fly once a month from New Haven to Chicago just for Lulu's violin lessons.

Despite their fame as the world's leading string pedagogues, their multiple honours received from the White House, the Vamoses had no airs. They would go to student parties and hang out with them. Students lived in their house and drove their car. The Vamoses took in students not just because of their playing skills but because of the chemistry they had with them. Their whole life seemed to revolve around their students.

It sounded just like what I needed: An instant family. I met the Vamoses in Minnesota. They were going to join the faculty at Oberlin Conservatory. I knew that I wanted to better myself, so I auditioned for the Artist Diploma programme at Oberlin and, joy of joys, I was offered a full scholarship. Everyone thought I was crazy to leave New York and start all over again in a little town in the Mid-West, but somehow, deep inside me, I knew that this was the right thing to do.

It turned out to be one of the best decisions I ever made.

54

WINNERS AND LOSERS

After all the hustle and bustle of New York, Oberlin seemed quaint. It was a small college town in the American Midwest, with one Chinese restaurant and one movie theatre.[14] It was so small, I could walk to everything that was essential to me: the Chinese restaurant, a Subway, a diner called The Feve and a bakery where fresh muffins were sold. However, there were no fancy shopping malls the sort that I knew. For a hardcore Singaporean shopaholic, this seemed like a death sentence.

Compared to New York, Oberlin was cheap, real cheap. I no longer had to worry about making ends meet. Not only was everything affordable, but there also was precious little to buy. Maybe I could end up rich after all, I mused. For me, the big event of the week was to dress up in my finery and go to the supermarket.

Much to my surprise, I never felt happier. The experience was liberating.

---

14 To my knowledge, it still has only one movie theatre.

At the time, I was in my twenties and felt like a grand dame at Oberlin. The college was primarily for undergraduates. The British violinist Kathy Gowers became my best friend and practice buddy. She was as crazy as I was: she had moved from London for her Artist Diploma at Oberlin. Kathy and I pushed each other every inch of the way, mostly because the cold winters in Oberlin were impossible to face alone. It was the closest I came to being in Siberia (without getting arrested for political dissent and having to work in a salt mine).

In those frigid winter mornings, waking up to practise was a struggle. Kathy and I would meet at 9 am, fortify ourselves with local muffins, brace ourselves for the sub-zero arctic chill and head off to practise. We camped out in practice rooms that were side by side, and checked in with each other every hour or so to see that we hadn't died of hypothermia. After a hot lunch, we would diligently repeat the whole routine. I chalked up six to seven hours a day. I had never practised so much nor so consistently.

The library was the other place where I hid from the cold. I pored over journals and periodicals, got addicted to *The Strad* magazine, and became obsessed with violin technique. Kathy and I especially looked forward to reading the latest instalment of Simon Fischer's violin tips in *The Strad*. We just couldn't wait to get our hands on them and even had our secret stash of Simon Fischer jokes. "Have you heard from Simon lately?" we would tease each other, as if we had a crush on him!

In spite of the cold, it warmed my heart to be part of the Vamoses' extended musical family. Before Mrs Vamos, all my major teachers were men. Like Rosand and Brodsky, Mrs Vamos also carried on the tradition of Eugène Ysaÿe, having studied with Ysaÿe's disciple Louis Persinger. However, unlike my male teachers who had a more formal teaching approach, Mrs Vamos had a totally different kind of chemistry with her students. Beyond the one-hour weekly lesson, she embraced her students as if they were family. When I gave concerts in Cleveland as a run-through for competitions, she would drive with me to provide support, like a concerned parent. When I made my debut in London, she came along. We even travelled together to Israel for summer festivals where we practised in bomb shelters (with bombs flying overhead) and ate at cooperatives. Outside of music, we bonded over girly things like painting our nails or going shopping together. She opened her home to students, invited us to stay over and join in their Thanksgiving dinners. We did everything together and there was a great esprit de corps among students in her class. It was a lot of fun.

Almita and Roland Vamos (seated)

The Vamoses taught as a husband-and-wife team. They were amazingly gifted teachers who had the knack for building your confidence no matter what level you were at, and for making you perform beyond your best. My tuition scholarship covered a weekly lesson with Mrs Vamos, who was my principal teacher, and because Mr Vamos generously let me sit in his classes for free, I got two lessons a week for the price of one!

For the whole of one semester, I practised and played in lessons for Mrs Vamos and diligently observed Mr Vamos teach. They were miracle workers of the violin. They took in students, fixed their problems, gave them hope and a sense of direction. The results were astounding. Practically every week, at least one of their students would return with a win from a competition. I was truly amazed.

Then it dawned on me what their secret was.

58 They had so much experience that they could instinctively put their fingers on just two or three things that could make the biggest difference to a student's playing. They knew exactly how to motivate students to put in the hard work with a willing heart, nose to the grindstone, day in and day out.

Like dieting or going to the gym.

Unfortunately, my previous efforts at dieting and going to the gym had not been entirely successful. Left to my own devices – especially when in the presence of chocolate – my cave(wo)man instincts get the better of me. My brain resets to Stone Age mode: Eat and Store, food is hard to come by. The sight of exercise equipment shuts down my brain to "Save Energy" mode. (Sit-ups? I'll just sit down for a while and think about it.) My body naturally opts out of energy-intensive habits just in case I needed the calories to run from a marauding sabre-toothed tiger. My cavemen ancestors would have been proud of me. And so it was, that the gym machines I ordered with grave resolve (typically after New Year binging) collected dust, until I discovered a personal trainer who loved to crack the whip. All that whip-cracking actually worked pretty well, and it was not long before I was able to show off my biceps when I played.

I digress.

There is little doubt that I am a 21st century violinist with Stone Age instincts, and a masochist to boot. I needed to feel the pinch of paying someone to put me to task before I would work through mundane exercises, like etudes and scales. These are the musical equivalent of crunches and weights – who enjoys them? But if you have the fortitude to work through them without giving up, there is no doubt that you will be able to see (and hear) the difference with every passing day.

So I hunkered down to some serious work and paid for extra lessons with Mr Vamos out of my own hard-earned pocket-money. The thought that I could still improve even as I was inching closer to my thirties was encouraging, so I decided to try for a competition. In fact, just before I went to Oberlin, I had signed up for the Wieniawski International Violin Competition, since one of the first showpieces Dad taught me was by the Polish violinist and composer Henryk Wieniawski.

The competition took place in the Polish city of Poznan. While there, I met a truly memorable person: a taxi driver. As with most taxi drivers, he was chatty, and when he saw my violin, asked, "Are you taking part in the competition? What pieces are you playing?" I mentioned one of Wieniawski's concertos. He surprised me by asking if I was doing flying staccato in a certain passage in the concerto. My jaw dropped.

Flying staccato is a fancy technique that violinists use to show off the fireworks they can perform with their right hand. Wieniawski was one of its most brilliant exponents, and he pushed the envelope further with dizzyingly rapid flying staccato passages in many of his works. It takes years for violinists to master, and was not a subject you would expect to crop up in casual conversation. I was seriously impressed. So proud are the Poles of their musical heritage that even their taxi drivers know about flying staccato.

If a taxi ride was the highlight of my trip, no prizes for guessing how far I got in the competition. The brutal truth is that I stumbled through to the second round before being unceremoniously booted out. As a consolation, I was given a Commemorative Diploma with Honours. I could not figure out what was worthy of commemoration.

I felt terribly dejected until Wanda Wiłkomirska, a famous Polish violinist who was one of the judges, came to talk to me. A beautiful, statuesque woman with high cheekbones, she cut an enigmatic figure. I was surprised that she approached me. Typically, after a competition, only the winners get any attention.

"You played really well," she said. "You should stay on and play some concerts around Poland." When she spoke, she had a way of making you feel like you were the only one who mattered. She made me feel special, and I liked her very much. Those few words changed my outlook and spurred me on. She made me look at competitions in a different way. It's not the winning but the effort that counts, and how fast you pick yourself up after defeat. To this day, I remember her words of encouragement.

Toughened by my Polish experience, I decided to try again.

In the summer of 1994, I went to the International Tchaikovsky Competition in Moscow. The programme was tremendously difficult, and I was eliminated in the first round. I felt like I had been punched in the gut a second time. Ever the sensitive musician, losing a second competition in a row burst my emotional faucet.

I have always counted Rachmaninoff and Tchaikovsky among my favourite composers, and love playing their works, so much so that a music critic once described me as "a full-fledged adopted Russian". Fuelled by the outpouring of emotions that is so characteristic of Russian music, my most negative passions spewed out. Suddenly, everything around me was coated in dark and depressing hues.

Russia then was in a mess (will I be sent to Siberia and made to work in a salt mine for saying this?). My newfound Russian friend, the pianist who had accompanied me when I played, introduced me to her husband. He was a high-flying aerospace scientist, but even he struggled to make ends meet. At a local bar, kids splashed out on drinks that cost the same as they did in Manhattan, while on the street outside a babushka[15] begged for pennies. The contrast was as crazy as it was cruel. I had never seen anything like it. It was my first time witnessing economic disparity up-close. And I didn't like it. Deeply affected and disillusioned, I thought, *What's the point of it all?*

The encouraging words of Wanda Wiłkomirska were long gone, and I did something I had never done before: I boycotted the violin for the next three months. I didn't even take it out of its case.

It was a low point in my career.

After three months of moping, I began to miss it. For someone who has played the violin since the tender age of seven, it becomes an important

61

---

15 Russian for "an elderly woman".

part of your life, like a childhood sweetheart or an intimate and trusted friend. For just how long, really, did I think I could stay away?

Meekly, I began making friends with it again. Be sure, a violin makes for a jealous lover. It needs to be touched and fondled and played with. If you don't spend time with it, it protests in its own way, not giving you the sound (and pleasure) you want.

Around this time, I discovered that the Second Henryk Szeryng International Violin Competition was taking place in the fall. Many of the set pieces were already in my repertoire. Mrs Vamos encouraged me to have another go.

Initially, I just wanted a goal to work towards, a way to force myself to start practising again. Then, the more I practised, the more I realised there was so much to catch up on. I stepped up my game. I never worked so hard in my life. It was the first time I practised 10 hours a day.

My roommate at Oberlin, the pianist Lois Hobbs, was instrumental (if you will excuse the pun) in egging me on. She knew how daunting it was to prepare for a competition – not unlike preparing for the Olympics. Lois was ingenious, and created incentives for me to see the light at the end of the tunnel. She knew that I was lusting after two things: a Stradivarius violin and a sofa set. So, she cut out a picture of a Strad and pasted it on the fridge. Then she pasted a photo of a sofa set on the TV. Every time I wanted to steal a break, I would see the sofa stuck on the screen. If I headed to the kitchen for a snack, the Strad-on-the-fridge would be staring back at me. And so, it was that I had found myself another personal trainer to curb my Stone Age instincts. The prize money was US$15,000. To get my Strad, I had to win this competition.

The competition was in Mexico and it went on for three weeks. The first round started in October. I progressed through the preliminaries, and when I reached the finals, a friend asked me, "You will definitely be in the top three. Would you be satisfied if you got the bronze medal?"

Of course I said no.

"Would you be satisfied if you got a silver?"

NO!

I was determined to win this time. I didn't want to go through the lows I had experienced during the Tchaikovsky Competition. I was sick and tired of being a loser.

When, finally, I clinched the Gold Medal of the Henryk Szerying International Violin Competition, victory tasted oh-so-sweet. It was a twist of fate that in the final round I won it with Tchaikovsky's Violin Concerto. I had practised it so many times for the earlier two competitions that I could do it with my eyes closed. Perhaps, as they say, it was third time lucky.

With the gold medal safely in my hands, Wanda Wiłkomirska's words came to me again: What matters most is how you pick yourself up again. You'll never know when success is right around the corner.

In hindsight, I have the Vamoses and Oberlin to thank for winning the Henryk Szeryng. There was simply nothing else to do there but lock myself up and practise. And even then, I needed mental tricks and my dear teachers and buddies to help me focus. Honestly, if you asked me if I could do it again, I couldn't. And that's why I moved to Chicago.

Gold Medal at the Second Henryk Szeryng International Violin Competition

Siow

Lee

Chin

❝ Here was a
lark that ascended
with utmost grace
and sang in the
loveliest of voices. ❞

The Cleveland Plain Dealer

ography by Dr Siow Yew Nam

Growing up
in Singapore
and America

(above) At home with my parents
and brothers Yew Nam
(with tie) and Yew Mun.

(right) Backstage with Yew
Nam and my parents during my
first concert as soloist with the
Singapore Symphony Orchestra.

(left) With friends from Raffles Girls' School.

(below) At the Curtis Institute of Music with my teacher Jascha Brodsky.

" Lee Chin is a violinist of outstanding talent, a thoughtful and serious musician, possessing both elegance and distinct temperament. "

Jascha Brodsky,
Efrem Zimbalist Chair,
Curtis Institute of Music

(left) My parents at my Curtis graduation.

Around the world with my violin

Charleston, SC, USA: Home of Spoleto Festival USA, where I co-founded the Charleston Music Fest. *(Photo courtesy of CharlestonMag.com. Photography by Peter Frank Edwards)*

Chile: As soloist performing the Bruch Violin Concerto with the Orquesta Sinfónica de Chile. *(Photo courtesy of Orquesta Sinfónica de Chile)*

Ukraine: In the train, on my way to perform Samuel Barber's Violin Concerto with the Kiev and Lviv Philharmonic Orchestra.

Singapore: Homecoming concert with cellist Qin Li-Wei and pianist Bernard Lanskey, who is also Director of the Yong Siew Toh Conservatory of Music, National University of Singapore. *(Photo courtesy of Yong Siew Toh Conservatory of Music)*

Washington DC, USA: Masterclass at the Levine School of Music.

Singapore: Performing at my country's National Day Parade, 1999. *(Photo courtesy of Singapore Press Holdings)*

Adventures in China

THE GREAT WALL, BEIJING

LIJIANG

SHANGHAI

SUZHOU

(Photography by Kevin Bourque)

Giving back

Fundraising for the President's Challenge: Cheque presentation to then-President of Singapore S.R. Nathan on the 130th anniversary of my alma mater, Raffles Girls' School.
(Photo courtesy of Raffles Girls' School)

Playing big sister to RGS students: A well-deserved pat on the back for soloist Giam Yue Ling after our performance of Vivaldi's Concerto for Four Violins with the RGS String Ensemble.
(Photo courtesy of Raffles Girls' School)

Meeting then-President of Singapore Wee Kim Wee at the fundraising concert for the Singapore Chinese Girls' School.

With Singapore Deputy Prime Minister Teo Chee Hean, Senior Minister of State (Ministry of National Development & Ministry of Trade and Industry) Lee Yi Shyan and friends from Keppel Corporation, City Sponsor of Oberlin Orchestra's debut in Singapore.
(Photo courtesy of Keppel Corporation)

“ The experience with Ms Siow was most precious because it inspired me to throw my heart into my musical journey with the diligence of a man whose life depends on it. ”

Neville Athenasius Ang,
SNYO member

Masterclass with Singapore National Youth Orchestra (SNYO): Coaching Neville Athenasius Ang on the Mendelssohn Violin Concerto before his solo debut with the SNYO. *(Photography by Rachel Toh)*

Sharing the finer points of Dvořák's music with Edward Koay and music students at a masterclass in Raffles Institution. *(Photography by Dr Siow Yew Nam)*

With the budding young artists I coached at a masterclass presented by the Ministry of Education for Music Elective Programme students.

Kicking off Singapore's Golden Jubilee celebrations at the 2015 City of London Festival with my solo recital in the City's oldest and most atmospheric church, St Bartholomew the Great.
(Photo courtesy of Vicky Flores, City of London Festival 2015)

As chair of the jury of the inaugural China-Singapore Young Talents Competition with Singapore Consulate-General in Shanghai Ong Siew Gay (third from left), Suzhou Industrial Park Administrative Committee Chairman Barry Yang (fifth from left) and the prizewinners.

Performing alongside my students from Soochow University School of Music at the first "Absolute Violin" concert in Suzhou Industrial Park's Youth and Children Centre.

With students from Soochow University School of Music.

With students from College of Charleston.

66 A distinguished
cultural asset
of international
stature. 99

American Record Guide

(Photography by Alan Lim)

AROUND THE WORLD WITH MY VIOLIN

At the age of nine or 10, I went up to my mother and asked, "When can I start wearing a bra?" I was a little kid trying to grow up fast, worried that my boobs would get in the way of my violin playing.

Thankfully, adolescence didn't stop me from performing.

In fact, it was while performing for the American violinist Aaron Rosand, who, as I have earlier mentioned, came to Singapore to perform as guest soloist with the Singapore Symphony Orchestra, that I was offered the chance to go to the Curtis Institute in the US to study under him. To a girl from Clementi, going to Curtis meant living and breathing in the same air as the musical legends who had once studied there. Who could turn down such an opportunity? In addition, the itch to travel was in me, and I had wanted very much to scratch it. I was a curious soul and keen to see the world. While I was at Raffles Girls' School (RGS), some of my friends would return from holidays with stories of trips to faraway places: of the food they ate and of the many amazing things they had seen. I had only read about such things in books, and I wanted to experience them for myself.

The world seemed like an awfully big place, but my violin had offered me a ticket to an adventure- and glamour-filled life (or so I thought). Winning the Henryk Szeryng Competition allowed me to travel to far-flung, exotic destinations. With the prize came a South American tour and concerts in Europe to follow. I had several managers on several different continents at that time.

There was this one particular manager who was always late with my fees. I racked my brains for hours trying to think how to deal with this problem, but we hadn't been taught how to deal with money collection at school. He gave excuse after excuse until finally I had had enough. The time had come for him to realise that you don't mess with an RGS girl!

He had scheduled me to play Bruch's Scottish Fantasy in Germany. I have given so many concerts that often, I cannot remember what piece I played where, but this concert is vividly etched in my memory because the opening bars of the Fantasy calls for an assured and deeply penetrating melody with an unwavering voice. One needs nerves of steel to carry this melody. Faced with the thought of confronting my manager, my mind was far from the Zen-like stoicism that the Bruch demanded.

I had no choice. It was my bread and butter. He owed me money and I didn't want to do another gig without being paid. There was nothing else for it. I wouldn't play a single note unless he paid me *NOW*! Just minutes before I was due on stage, against his better instincts, he relented and passed me a huge wad of cash.

With that, came another problem: *where was I to put it?* After considering for about 30 seconds, the only thing I could think of was to stuff the money in my bra. With padded bra and violin in hand, I stormed on stage to take on the Bruch.

Although very well endowed that night, I was trembling with rage. I had summoned up all my courage to stand up to my manager, and now I had to switch to a calmer mood and coax the meditative melodies of the Bruch from my violin. My heart was racing – not from nerves but from fear.

Will my dress give way and spill the cash out?

Little did the audience know the load I was carrying! Being an artist may seem glamorous, but often there is far more to it than meets the eye – far, far more.

More drama followed me to my London debut at the Royal Albert Hall. The Royal Albert is to London what Carnegie Hall is to New York. The Beatles, Eric Clapton and Sting have belted out their hits to frenzied fans in that hallowed hall, and it was there that an English manager invited me to play a benefit concert with the Royal Philharmonic Orchestra for the Elton John AIDS Foundation. Elton John himself was in the Royal Box that night. Just before my turn came, Sir Simon Rattle stepped up to the podium to conduct Elgar's Enigma. In the world of classical music, it didn't get more British than this.

Among all the pomp and ceremony, was this star-struck newbie from Singapore. It is one thing to play as a soloist, but to be featured in an all-star line-up was something else altogether. Here I was, about to perform to one of the most sophisticated audiences in the world. How the heck did this happen? I pinched myself to make sure I wasn't dreaming.

It hurt; I wasn't dreaming.

Nervously, I checked out the hall from backstage. The 5000-seater hall was packed to the rafters, but try as I may, I couldn't spot even one member of the Siow Lee Chin Fan Club. I scanned the hall for the contingent from Oberlin, heartened that I could count on their support – even though I

67

could count them on the fingers of one hand. The Vamoses plus my good friends Marci Rich, Ariane Sletner and Kathy Gowers had specially flown 3,763 miles just to hear me play. Although I couldn't see them, I knew they were there and I knew I had better make their trip worth their while.

Mrs Vamos had helped me fine-tune and polish the passionate Carmen Fantasy, which I had first learnt from Jascha Brodsky when I was a student at Curtis. This was the very piece (Efrem Zimbalist's[16] famous transcription) I chose to play that night. Besides teaching me how to pull out all the stops to dazzle the audience with Carmen's musical pyrotechnics, Mr Brodsky had enthralled me with a lesson on life and love. I still remember him translating to me the lyrics of the famous French aria sung by the beautiful gypsy Carmen:

Love is a rebellious bird
that nobody can tame,
and you call him quite in vain
if it suits him not to come
nothing helps, neither threat nor prayer.

The bird you thought you had caught
beat its wings and flew away
love stays away, you wait and wait;
when least expected, there it is!

16 Efrem Zimbalist was an internationally renowned concert violinist, composer, teacher, conductor and director of the Curtis Institute of Music. His pupils included such distinguished musicians as Oscar Shumsky, Joseph Silverstein, as well as my teachers Aaron Rosand and Jascha Brodsky.

I thought the Carmen Fantasy would have sufficient fireworks to warm up the reserved Brits and for visual impact, I wore a red Armani dress. I knew this to be important. As the saying goes: we listen with our eyes.

And *of course*, like most Singaporean girls, I like dressing up.

The audience applauded politely when I stepped on stage. I was determined to win them over with my fiery rendition of Carmen, and when I had finished playing, much to my relief, the audience responded enthusiastically; there were even a few cheers. Perhaps the SLC Fan Club had gained a few new members? (Elton John told me later, ever so graciously, that he was a fan. But I hadn't the nerve to ask him for the joining fee!)

After my performance, I quickly changed out of my gown because Spanish diva Montserrat Caballé and Italian tenor Andrea Bocelli were lined up to perform after me and I was eager to hear them sing. Meanwhile, a drama had broken out backstage. The two feisty singers had had a tiff! The upshot was that Caballé and Bocelli cancelled the duet that was supposed to end the concert.

At the very last minute, I was asked if I could fill the gap! Could I do an encore? Put on the spot, I was dumbfounded and mumbled a feeble excuse, "But... I've already changed out of my dress." It was not one of my finest moments. Aspiring musicians train for years waiting for such a break. To this day, I kick myself for missing this opportunity. What had happened to the kiasu me?

As it happened, Andrea Bocelli went out alone and sang the finale. In spite of the little spat, he sang beautifully. It still makes me wince whenever I recall this. I had paid the price to learn an important lesson: the biggest

69

chances come at the most unexpected times. Lady Luck was as capricious as Cupid was, and Carmen's lyrics became painfully real to me: "you wait and wait; when least expected, there it is!" To take advantage of Lady Luck, you've got to be 100 per cent ready all the time. There are no exceptions, no excuses.

Soloist spots on the international stage are as sought after as leading roles in Hollywood blockbusters. Plum roles are few and far between. For every available position, there are hundreds, if not thousands, of others waiting in the wings. The blunt reality is that a career in classical music is as dicey as a career in Hollywood. In the end, it often boils down to not how good you are, but who you know. Sadly, the old boys' network controls the music world in the same way that it does the corporate world.

Had I known what I was getting myself into, I might have been more apprehensive about pursuing a solo career. But then again, if it was easy, everybody would be doing it, and where's the fun in that? It may have been the folly of youth, but my secret weapon was that I was naïve. Growing up, Dad had kept telling me that if I put my mind to it, anything was possible. He gave me a precious gift – the belief in myself. Innocence is truly the most powerful arsenal that the young have.

In America, I was wrapped up and inspired by the Great American Dream. The idea that anyone could achieve success if they worked at it resonated with me. I was not born with a silver spoon, and could not count on generations of family connections to launch my career. Americans don't wait for things to be handed out to them, and so I learnt to speak up and just as importantly, to be proactive.

Young, foolish and fresh out of school, I returned to Singapore after graduation, hoping to contribute to its burgeoning music scene. We were a young nation and our pool of musicians was relatively small. I saw how countries like Japan celebrated their home-grown talents like Midori, and I thought Singapore should also showcase its own artists and that which was unique to us. It's great to be able to bring in international acts to perform in Singapore, but if all the juicy soloist roles keep going to foreigners, how can Singaporean artists get a chance to grow?

Once, while in Singapore catching up with friends, I learnt that the Dallas Symphony would be in town to perform in the Singapore Festival of Arts (now known as the Singapore International Festival of Arts). Under its Music Director Eduardo Mata, the Dallas Symphony had grown into one of the most successful American orchestras, and Mata himself was going to conduct. Ever the optimist, I asked, "Who's the soloist?" I was, of course, hoping that a Singaporean would be given the chance, and being naïve little me, I thought it should be none other than... *moi*! I was relatively unknown back then, but this was precisely the time when an artist needed a break.

I had no idea at the time just how hard this would be. I knocked on door after door until my knuckles bled, before realising that this honour was not going to be handed to me on a silver platter. By chance, the Mexican Ambassador to Singapore, H.E. Manuel Uribe Castañeda, happened to hear about what I had in mind. He loved the violin, had been to my concerts, and thought it was a great idea. He knew the conductor Eduardo Mata and offered to be matchmaker.

I don't know exactly how it happened, I just know that the stars must have aligned just at the right moment, and as they did, so the doors opened. For the second time in my life, an ambassador had been instrumental in

71

Performing in Singapore with the Dallas Symphony conducted by Eduardo Mata. I was the first Singaporean to perform as soloist with a visiting, internationally-acclaimed orchestra. *(Photo courtesy of Singapore Press Holdings)*

stepping forward to help a young, unknown artist. To this day, I have great faith in what ambassadors can do.

Thus, it was to my delight that in 1992, I was invited to be the soloist with the Dallas Symphony under the "Homecoming Series" introduced by Singapore's National Arts Council. It was the first concert by a visiting internationally acclaimed orchestra to feature a Singaporean soloist. For me, it was like a dream come true.

That was my first big break. Like Carmen's prophetic words about falling in love, these things happen when you least expect them. I am a firm believer that young people should be encouraged to dream big and take concrete steps to advocate their causes. I learnt that along the way, there will be the unavoidable naysayers, but hard work, patience and perseverance could often translate into lucky breaks. I was fortunate to have met generous and kind sponsors who believed in me and gave their support.

Like the eager beaver I was, I said yes to almost everything that was offered to me. I would fly 40,000 kilometres from Asia to America and back within 7 days, and still have reserves from all the adrenalin swimming around my body. It was while I was on one of these crazy schedules that I was slotted to solo with the Houston Symphony. Zipping in and out of the city with only one rehearsal, there was barely enough time to say hello to Maestro Andreas Delfs. The concert took place in an outdoor theatre in the middle of summer, with an audience of 5,000. I sweated like I had never sweated before, with only adrenalin to keep me going. When it wore off – as it always does – I was left not only with dehydration but also with a chronic bad back. Who would have thought that playing the violin could be such back-breaking work?

From early on, I made it a point to schedule masterclasses in schools or universities wherever I played. No matter how tired I felt, working with young people always recharged my batteries. Perhaps I had inherited the teaching bug from Dad. In the passionate faces of young musicians, I saw myself. They and their parents invariably asked the same questions: "Is it possible to make a living in music? How does one become a soloist? What did you do?"

When I was at school, I had asked myself the very same questions. The running joke was that to succeed in the music industry, you had to be male, Jewish and gay. *Oh dear*, I thought to myself. *I'm female, Chinese and straight.* The odds were stacked heavily against me. So I turned to my teacher Jascha Brodsky for some much needed advice.

73

Mr Brodsky made three suggestions:

1. Win a competition.
2. Appear on the front page of every newspaper.
3. Get the Rockefellers to be your parents.

It seemed impossible, but being the Type A personality I was, I decided to give them a shot. I was able to put a check against Number One, only to discover that it wasn't an exclusive club – many others were in it too. Number Two remained elusive (and still does), while Number Three was a biological impossibility. Clearly, scoring one out of three wasn't enough. Since my bank balance wasn't growing as fast as the bills were rolling in, I improvised and came up with my own survival guide.

1. Be realistic and resourceful

There is so much more to a performance career than meets the eye. Playing well is just the first step. As the saying goes, "It takes a village to raise a child." Similarly, it takes a whole network of support to see an artist from the practice room to the concert hall.

Young artists must be realistic. Don't wait for things to happen. Managers are simply not going to come knocking on your door, especially in the beginning. In the initial stages of my career, I had to arrange my own concerts. In fact, some of my biggest gigs came from my own efforts.

Start with those you know: your peers and professors. Seek their help and advice, and keep in touch with your alma mater, colleagues, including conductors you've worked with. Some maestros may seem like demi-gods but believe me, they're also human.

2. Be ready for Lady Luck, and take every gig seriously

Glamorous as it may seem, a classical soloist probably faces one of the fewest job openings in the world. How often do you see an advertisement for "Soloist" in the job ads? Not very often, right? If there were a ranking for job scarcity, soloist-hopefuls would probably come second to astronauts. Remember the time when more than 200,000 applied to fill around 20 spots to fly to Mars? The competition is almost as fierce for soloists.

In the case of a young artist, every gig is precious – even those that pay nothing. This was certainly true for me.

As a student, I went to Aspen several times. Every year, this little town in the Colorado Mountains transforms itself from ski-central in winter to music camp-central in summer. Young musicians make their pilgrimage from all corners of the globe to be mentored by the likes of cellist Yo-Yo Ma and other star faculty and perform in orchestras alongside them. I did my share of masterclasses with pedagogues, such as Juilliard violin faculty Dorothy DeLay, and also played in concerts. Sometimes, I would just chill out with friends. While other times, I would busk on the streets.

From busking, I made more new friends and when I went back to New York, I got invited to more gigs. One thing led to another and one fine day, I landed an invitation to play in a benefit concert for the New York Public Library, with former US Secretary of State Henry Kissinger and then US First Lady Barbara Bush in the audience.

The dots only connect with hindsight, but we don't have that advantage when we are taking our first steps. It's hard to predict where life will lead us to next. Take every performance seriously and be professional, even if it's a gig on the street in a small town. Never in my wildest dreams could I have imagined that from busking I could get to play for Barbara Bush and Henry Kissinger.

3. Put it on paper

It's great to have dreams and aspirations, but nothing's going to happen unless you're committed. I have always believed in putting things down on paper. Whether you scribble it in a notebook or save it on a computer, there's something about having it written down that holds you to it. Every year, it has become a tradition for me to write down 10 goals as my New Year resolutions.

To bring my head down from the clouds, I try to refine this list to things that I can realistically work towards. I may wish to be the greatest violinist on earth, but that won't get me anywhere. So to get cracking, set attainable goals, such as, "I want to have 30 concerts next year, which means I need to learn 5 concertos this year."

This way, it becomes more tangible and not so impossible.

4. Break it down

If what you want to do seems really challenging, make it less daunting by breaking it down into smaller parts. This is how I tackle a difficult piece. If I try to learn a big concerto with many difficult parts all at once, it can be overwhelming. Breaking it into smaller parts helps to smoothen the way.

Supposing you want to tackle a tough three- or four-bar passage. First, break it down into the right and left hand. If it's predominantly difficult on the left hand, then know exactly what's going on in the right hand, and then combine it.

Trying to fix everything at one go can be overwhelming. But if you work out one kink at a time, things will soon start humming along nicely.

5. Be relevant

Be creative about how you get your gigs. Look around and find ways to be relevant. Volunteer.

Initially, it was difficult to get all the concerts I had hoped for. Since I had time on my hands, I would play at nursing homes. New York can be a lonely place, and I felt deeply for the elderly folks living out their twilight years in these homes.

One incident has stayed with me all these years. I was at a nursing home playing Sarasate's Zigeunerweisen, a virtuosic piece based on Hungarian folk music. After I had wrapped up the performance, an old lady came up to me with tears in her eyes. She clutched my hand and said, "Thank you, you made me remember my hometown as a young girl."

Being a soloist can tend to make you a narcissist (*you mean the spotlight doesn't follow me when I walk off stage?*) and this encounter has kept me grounded. The fact that my music could make someone's day, made it all seem worthwhile. Little did I realise that instead of just being the giver, I was also the recipient. I thought I was doing something for these elderly folks, which I was, yet inadvertently, playing for them also allowed me to hone my skills and learn how to connect with an audience. It cuts both ways.

77

Think outside the box, don't limit yourself. As a young person, there are many opportunities to hone your skills and to contribute.

6. Don't be afraid, be super prepared

Gary Graffman, a renowned pianist who has nurtured virtuosos like Lang Lang and Yuja Wang, was the President of the Curtis Institute when I was there as a student. Once, he pulled me aside and whispered to me one of the most valuable pieces of advice a young soloist could get.

"If you're playing a certain piece for the first time, don't let on that it's your first time. Be confident and don't show you're afraid. Otherwise, the conductor will eat you for lunch."

So, what can we do to overcome our nerves?

The trick is to build confidence through performance practice so that when the big moment comes, you're something of a veteran. For instance, if my students have a concert at 8 pm, I would advise them to arrange several small performances at exactly 8 pm in the weeks running up to the actual event, dress up as they would for the concert, invite a couple of friends over so there is an audience, and have a recording device ready. Even the act of playing to an iPhone gives one a sense of heightened awareness. A recording allows us to hear ourselves (and our mistakes) objectively and critically. To this day, I still use one.

The key is to trick our brains and manage our nerves by recreating the scenario as many times as possible. Be critical and serious in the practice room. Be super-prepared so that when the big day comes, we can let go and enjoy the moment.

7. Don't be shy

Living in America taught me to speak up. From an Asian point of view, this is often misconstrued as being brash. As in many other areas, there is a line that you are continually hopping over when exposed to two different cultures. It helps that I am a people person. Still, I went through the struggles many young artists face, especially in finding a good manager to promote me and arrange for more gigs.

As part of my survival skills, I learnt to develop a thick skin. After I won the Artists International Competition in New York, I got a copy of *Musical America*. In the pre-Internet days, this was a thick go-to directory that listed all the artist management companies in the country. I pored over it, wrote to all the managers and sent out letters. Of course, a plethora of polite rejections came scurrying back. I soldiered on.

79

For sensitive souls, this can be a tough time. But after the first few rejections, I learnt not to take them personally.

When I was due to perform my debut at Carnegie Weill Recital Hall, I sent out invitations to some of the managers. One of these managers actually came and, joy of joys, decided to sign me. I had landed my first management contract.

Rejections are common. We all encounter them. Don't let these deter you.

8. Articulate your passion and find common interests

People love to witness passion, and generally like to support worthy causes. If you have a dream or passion for something, don't be afraid to articulate it. You might just come across someone who shares your interest, is as passionate about it as you are, and is willing to be in your corner to champion your cause.

When I was living in New York, I got acquainted with several instrument dealers. One of them was Jacques Francais, whom *The New York Times* described as "a dealer in classical string instruments who with a glance could authenticate a Stradivarius worth millions and then often match it with its next player".

Jacques had a charming French accent and a permanent twinkle in his eye. Musicians loved to visit him. His shop on 57th Street was more like a doctor's clinic. All the major artists, from Isaac Stern to Joshua Bell, would go there to adjust their instruments and get them in tip-top shape for that extra boost they required before an important concert.

80

With Jacques Francais

Jacques was so very sweet to me. He saw that I was not only a good violinist but also that we shared a passion for music and fine instruments. He helped me by hosting a house concert in his beautiful apartment overlooking Central Park, so that more people might get to know me. Once, he loaned me a magnificent Stradivarius violin that had been played by the late Wolfgang Schneiderhan, an Austrian violinist and concertmaster of the Vienna Philharmonic Orchestra. I performed the Mendelssohn Violin Concerto on that Strad at the Ludwigsburg International Music Festival in Germany.

When I heard the recording, I was amazed at the beauty of the instrument's inherent voice. I finally understood the importance of an instrument to a musician. Sadly, Jacques passed away in 2004. I am forever grateful for his support, especially at the time when I was starting out in my career.

81

9. Be open to meeting new people

Many of us seldom venture beyond our little circles and comfort zones, for it certainly takes effort to do so. I encourage my students to be curious and be open to meeting new people. Learn to make small talk, and venture into topics that may not be related to your field. Life is full of serendipitous surprises. You never know whom you may meet next.

At one of my concerts in Italy, I met a photographer who asked if he could photograph me. *Oh dear*, I thought, *is he one of these guys I had heard about? Those who are in fact serial killers but who moonlight as photographers so they can ravish young female violinists from Singapore?*

None of it.

He was Beppe Lopetrone, a professional fashion photographer who had photographed Sophia Loren and Claudia Schiffer. He was incredibly generous – not only did he bring in his make-up artist from Milan to glamour me up, he did the photo shoot for free. Since then, I have never underestimated the power of a wonderfully taken photograph. (Yes, people were visual creatures – myself included – long before the age of selfies.) What a huge blessing that chance encounter turned out to be.

Spot the difference:

Before   After
(Photography by Beppe Lopetrone)

10. Smell the roses and soak in the mountains

Many of my students can get so immersed in the violin that they don't have enough time to enjoy other activities. To some extent, I was guilty of this in my younger days too. If I had to do it all over again, I would take more time off to see the sights, go to the museums, listen to the operas. Reading about these things on the Internet doesn't count.

I remember vividly what the great American-Norwegian violinist Camilla Wicks told me. One of the first female international soloists, she was famous for her interpretation of the Sibelius Violin Concerto, and on one occasion having performed with the composer himself sitting in the audience. I studied the Sibelius Concerto with her. One wintry morning, during a break in practise at her house in Washington State, she led me to the window and pointed to the snowy mountains in the far distance.

"Keep this image for Sibelius," she said.

Most composers gather inspiration from their milieu and from their experiences. Immerse yourself in the culture and feel of a place, meet people, fall in love and have your heart broken. These are the things that arm us with the layers of nuance that makes music come alive.

11. Go the extra mile

A list of 10 would have wrapped up my list nicely. But I have decided to throw in one more for perfectionists like me who like to go the extra mile. When I've done what I consider to be my best, I push myself another 10 per cent before I up the stakes again.

We are on a journey with no end. So get cracking!

ON BECOMING A TEACHER

The idea of teaching came to me out of the blue when I was in Chicago catching up with Mrs Vamos.

We were out shopping, looking at handbags and shoes, when she casually mentioned that she and Mr Vamos were planning a sabbatical, and they were looking for replacements to take over their classes at Oberlin Conservatory while they were away. Then she turned, slowly and thoughtfully, and looked at me at the exact same moment I turned, slowly and thoughtfully, and looked at her. A flash of inspiration – not unlike a bolt of lightning in a clear sky – connected us.

Eureka! Vamos! (Spanish for "Let's Go!" – rather apt, now that I think about it). The moment passed in a second, yet that second changed my life.

I embarked on teaching the way some people enter into an arranged marriage: settle down first, then fall head over heels in love later. When I was handed the keys to the job as visiting professor at Oberlin, I was barely older than some of the students I had to teach. And what a job it was! It was like being handed the keys to a Rolls-Royce to take your driving test in. The Vamoses were highly respected teachers, honoured by the White House, no less, and described by many as the "Pied Pipers of Oberlin". Talented students from all over the world knocked down their door to study with them. Their protégés read like a Who's Who of violin competition and Grammy Award winners: Rachel Barton Pine, Jennifer Koh, Sibbi Bernhardsson...

Mrs Vamos thought of everything right down to the smallest detail. For example, she wanted to be sure that things didn't get out of hand while they were away, so she thoughtfully assigned me to teach her predominantly female studio, while Sibbi, now violinist in the Grammy Award winning Pacifica Quartet, was assigned to teach Mr Vamos' predominantly male studio.

I had always assumed that I was too impatient to make a good teacher, and this assumption proved to be not too far off the mark. The nurturing Mrs Vamos, as always, came to my rescue and dished out her usual good advice. She said I was too strict, jumping right away on what I didn't like, while proclaiming with a shrill voice, "This is simply not right!"

With her guidance, I learnt some ground rules, the most important of which was to strike up a rapport with your students.

"First you must find something about their playing that you like," Mrs Vamos would explain. "Tell them what you like, then when you have them in your court, you can throw the ball back and teach them how to improve."

Inspired by Mrs Vamos, I decided that the first thing I should do in class was to sit in her chair, from where she doled out her pearls of wisdom as she taught. By sitting in her chair, I harboured the hope that such pearls of wisdom would come naturally to me too.

Perhaps the chair gave me a psychological edge, because I soon learnt how to encourage my students and win them over in the way it had been explained to me.

85

Carrying on the musical tradition of Eugène Ysaÿe and Henryk Wieniawski
(Photo courtesy of College of Charleston)

"I feel this is a piece you can play really well," I would say after listening to a piece or a passage, "but you're not quite there yet. Perhaps you can try this. Let me demonstrate."

Then I would show them how to tackle the piece at hand.

I was pleasantly surprised how well I took to teaching and how I enjoyed helping my students grow musically. I have always loved problem-solving, and figuring out how to connect with each student was a challenge I relished. I remembered what the great Juilliard pedagogue Dorothy DeLay had taught me about communication.

As a student, I had played the Bruch Violin Concerto for her in a masterclass at the Aspen Music Festival. The opening of the Bruch is beautiful in its simplicity. It looks deceptively easy, yet to play it really well takes much artistry and depth of understanding. Some describe it as a sunrise unfolding; the sky gently awakening with beautiful light.

"But how would you teach this to a child who has never woken up early enough to see the sun rise?" Ms DeLay asked.

Dorothy DeLay's message was that teachers had to use analogies that their students could relate to. Another way to help a child appreciate the Bruch Concerto was to demonstrate how the placement of the bow on the string could create different colours and nuances. She was very methodical in teaching every step involved in making a beautiful line of music. Although I was still only in my teens at that time, her words stuck, and came even more alive when I started to teach.

The "light bulb" moments, when my students would suddenly "get it", were intoxicating. These moments in teaching are like the magical ones you experience in a performance, whenever the artist connects with the audience and both seem to breathe as one. These were the very moments I thrived on as an artist, and when I became a teacher, I instinctively knew that the most important way I could help my students was to teach them how to communicate, expressively. Technique, of course, was important, in the way that grammar is important in language. But I wanted my students to master musical technique in order to serve the music, to understand that it was a means to an end, so that they could deliver a powerful musical statement faultlessly, one which would resonate with their audience and move them to see that "sky gently awakening with beautiful light".

To their credit, most of the students were open to my suggestions. It was a revelation, even to me, that teaching could give me so much joy. As a student, I had pored over journals studying violin techniques. Helping students to figure out and fix their problems was a natural progression of this. Over time, I systematically developed my own set of exercises and etudes to solve a whole range of technical problems my students might encounter. I was very proud of myself.

In hindsight, watching Dad teach as I was growing up must have rubbed off on me. I remember how he would get excited when he discovered a new way of teaching something and how he would eagerly test his theories on me. Now, I had my own theories and methods to treat my own students' musical ailments. From a teaching perspective, I felt I was ready to deal with anything that was thrown at me.

Anything.

Until the day when a student approached me with a little problem: she had never kissed a boy.

"What is it like to kiss someone?" she asked.

"What does this have to do with the violin?" I replied.

No one had warned me that this was part of the deal. It then dawned on me that being a good teacher was about helping students grow, not just musically, but in all those other little ways, like kissing. Students look to a teacher for psychological and emotional support because making great music involves the whole being – mind, body and soul. If I'm teaching a student the violin, I also had to take care of his or her heart and mind too. I just didn't expect it would be such a tall order!

So, I rose to the challenge and told her, like I were an expert on the subject, that it was GREAT to kiss someone.

Teaching, I quickly figured out, was a two-way street. It wasn't just about me giving to the students. I found that teaching actually made me a better violinist, since I had to set a good example by demonstrating what

I expected of my students. Listening critically to myself play, analysing the structure and harmony of a piece, constantly working on intonation, posture and phrasing took on a new dimension because I had to walk the talk and earn my students' respect.

I tapped on these dynamics to make my students more proactive learners and listeners. Where possible, I would suggest they find a practice buddy to listen, observe and comment on each other's playing. It is easier to hear someone else's mistakes than your own. Invariably, students would zero in on areas that they themselves were preoccupied with. They learnt to be more aware of the problems they needed to fix.

The buddy system worked especially well if I knew there was someone a student fancied. If she wasn't forthcoming with practise, I would slyly plant the idea, "Why don't you ask him to be your practice buddy?" I was delighted to see some very positive outcomes... some of which may have even involved kissing.[17]

89

At times, the expectations of being a good teacher were overwhelming. People assume you know all the repertoire. I certainly didn't play all the pieces. No one did. The repertoire was too vast. But what if they found out I didn't have the answers to everything?

It was then that I remembered what Mr Rosand, my teacher at Curtis, used to do. Sometimes he would pick out a foreign word and throw it to me as a question, "What does this mean?" Music is full of Italian or German words. How was a teenager from Singapore expected to know what "lusingando" or "mit lebhafter steigerung" meant? I would be stumped. To

---

17 Full disclosure: I only encourage this for college-age students. Not applicable for those 18 and below.

my secret delight, most of my students found themselves in a spot too when I questioned them about the historical background of the pieces they were playing. I would thus proceed to give them a lecture about the importance of being informed musicians. Music was more than just about playing the notes. This mini lecture would take another five minutes off the class. (I have to admit it: as a professor, it was fun to climb on my moral high horse once in a while.)

I also dispensed many memorable lessons I gleaned from the musical legends with whom I had studied. One especially great violinist left an indelible impression on me: Sir Yehudi Menuhin. I was about 10 or 11 when I played for him at my first masterclass in Hong Kong.

After I finished, he asked me a question, which took me completely by surprise.

"Do you play baseball?"

I was expecting to hear his words of wisdom on how to play better, not to be thrown (excuse the pun) a question on baseball! These days, whenever I give masterclasses, I still love to surprise young musicians with the same question.

The point Menuhin was making was that there's so much to learn if we look at how sportsmen perform. Musicians seldom think of themselves as athletes, but playing the violin is as much a physical activity as it is an artistic one. We have to think, train and move like athletes. Menuhin had wanted me to work on sound projection. As violinists, we have to work on throwing our sound out to the audience, exactly like how a baseball player throws the ball: Prepare your stroke before playing the note. After your bow hits the strings, don't forget to follow through, so that the sound carries right through to the back of the hall. If you're playing in Carnegie

Hall, tell yourself, "I'm going to reach the 2,804th seat right at the back." In other words, play to the person seated at the very back of the hall.

When I tried my hand at archery, I learnt how critical concentration, endurance and discipline were. Most people think music is something we do for a bit of fun. None of it! It's bloody serious work! Just as an archer needs to focus in order to hit the target, a violinist needs to focus to get the perfect sound. In sports psychology, sportsmen train to let go of their errors in order to achieve a positive outcome. Similarly, on stage, musicians have to move on even when they stumble during a performance.

My semester as visiting professor at Oberlin flew by. I was thrilled with the wonderful feedback I received from my students and from Mrs Vamos. The sense of fulfilment I felt was immeasurable. Through years of interaction with Dad and other gifted teachers, I have evolved, along with my own philosophy for teaching the violin. I knew then that I wanted to combine my performing career with teaching, like many of my teachers at Curtis, Oberlin and Mannes had done.

I applied for teaching positions at several universities, and consequently was invited to a number of promising interviews. My first interview was unforgettable, most unfortunately. Emboldened by my success at Oberlin, I swaggered in with the regal air of a diva. So full of myself was I that – and you've probably guessed it already – I fell flat on my face. Needless to say, I didn't get the job, and my pride and my face still hurt when I think about it.

It was a humbling experience, which fortunately, didn't repeat itself. If nothing else, I am a fast learner, and I went on to secure several good offers, until eventually, with Mrs Vamos' blessing, I accepted the College of Charleston's invitation to join them as Professor of Violin and Director of

91

Strings Program. I wanted to be in a school where I could see things take root, watch them grow and develop into something significant. In addition, Charleston, with its balmy climate and green spaces, is a beautiful city. It reminded me of Singapore. I felt at home immediately.

When Mrs Vamos asked me what I wanted as a going away present, I didn't hesitate. I said I wanted her chair. When I packed my bags for the new job in Charleston, her chair came with me, and I've been sitting in it ever since.

OVERCOMING ADVERSITY

Eleanor Roosevelt once said, "Do one thing that scares you every day."

I'm not sure if my parents knew about Eleanor Roosevelt and what she had said, but the strand of DNA responsible for fear must have snapped before it was passed to me.

Growing up in America, I missed out on one of the most important coming-of-age rituals of American teenagers – learning to drive. In New York, I never got round to it because taking the subway was so much easier. At Oberlin, I finally learnt to drive a stick shift in an old Plymouth, which would start and stop as if it had a mind of its own. It wasn't the greatest of starts to my introduction into the world of automobiles, but at least I managed to get my licence.

After I moved to Chicago, I didn't get much practise driving around the windy city, since I spent more time in the air than I did on the ground. Then when I got the job at Charleston, I decided the time had come to buy a car and drive myself to South Carolina. The 963-mile drive could be done in 14 hours, so a few seasoned motorists had told me. As I was less seasoned, I thought I would split the journey over two days.

A friend helped me to buy a modest second-hand Nissan Maxima. Its golden colour was a little faded, but it was an automatic and much smoother than the rickety Plymouth. Sitting behind the wheel, I felt like a million bucks. Those being the days before the wonderful invention of the GPS, I armed myself with a good old-fashioned atlas, and with my Maxima filled to capacity with all my worldly belongings (clothes, books, music scores, LPs collected over 15 years, Mrs Vamos' chair and, of course, my trusty violin), I was all set to take on the world!

Well, the world as it was from Chicago to South Carolina.

Little did I know that even for seasoned drivers, just navigating the highways from Chicago to the interstate network, which would take me to South Carolina, could be a nightmare. There were many, Many, MANY lanes full of huge speeding trucks. (Did I mention that I am terrified of changing lanes?) Whenever there were vehicles close behind me, I stomped on the gas pedal instead of moving to the slower lane. When I finally got on the ramp to the interstate, my heart was racing twice as fast as the miles per hour I was travelling.

I crossed into the state of Indiana and through a maze of other highways and freeways, I swung by West Virginia and into Virginia where I spent the night in a small motel near to the town of Blacksburg.

Next morning, I was up early for the final lap through North and South Carolina into Charleston. Just as I began to chill to Stéphane Grappelli's jazzy tunes and when the world seemed a much sunnier place, I heard the piercing scream of a police siren. The scream drew closer and closer until it drowned out Mr Grappelli. Then an officer in blue appeared as if out of nowhere and waved me to the side. My heart was pounding.

Oh dear, I thought, *this is not a good way to start a new job.*

Lucky for me, the officer was nice. Seeing my bewildered look (the damsel in distress look I had spent years perfecting for just such moments) he asked, "Where are you going?"

I replied, "Driving to my new job in Charleston."

It appeared that I had gone over the speed limit.

"Please don't give me a ticket," I pleaded, "it's bad luck to be given a ticket before starting a new job."

He laughed at my excuse, probably already looking forward to telling the boys down at the station this new one. As it turned out, not only had I been speeding, but I had also gone off track and was driving the wrong way! He kindly escorted me back in the right direction, and, with a cheery wave, wished me good luck in my new job. Finally, after more than 20 hours, I found my way down south in one piece with no further brushes with the law.

95

This journey remains on record as the longest journey I have ever driven by myself.

The Maxima served me loyally for eight years, and when the time came to retire it, I was sorry to see it go. At the same time, I was thrilled to upgrade it for a spiffy silver BMW 3 series, equipped with all the state-of-the-art safety features the motor industry had invented. Even though I inherited Dad's frugal habits (and his looks, if I may add), I couldn't help but give myself this little reward. I loved my new toy! To me, it was perfect: from the way it looked and how well it handled the road. It didn't hurt that it came at just a fraction of the price it would have cost me in Singapore.

In the spring of 2012, the American String Teachers Association (ASTA) invited me to present at the National Conference in Atlanta, Georgia, about a five-hour drive from my home in Charleston. ASTA is one of the largest gatherings of string professionals in America, and it was a great honour to present to such a distinguished crowd of colleagues. I was eager to ignite some interest – and hopefully a little magic – on the seemingly mundane subject of "How to Practise Effectively". And to boot, I was looking forward to catching up with old friends in the Atlanta Symphony.

When I left Charleston, it was a beautiful sunny morning. I whistled to my favourite Grappelli CD as I drove along. Unlike the seven- and eight-lane Chicago highways, I only had to manage two lanes in South Carolina. I planned to drive to Columbia (a two-hour drive), park at my friend Jerry Dell's house, and hitch a ride from another friend who was also headed for Atlanta. We would finish the trip together and have some fun.

Unfortunately, I didn't get that far.

Somewhere near the town of Orangeburg, an 18-wheeler truck whizzed by at my shoulder, and in that split second, my car refused to go straight, even though I was not travelling fast. My brakes didn't seem to work.

Oh my God, I thought, *I'm going to die.*

I'm still not sure what exactly happened. Based on the damage to the car, it's likely I was hit on the passenger (right) side by the 18-wheeler.

One thing you should know about me is that I hate not being in control. Instinctively, I willed my car to veer towards the left. Miraculously, it moved towards the centre lane divider and hit the guardrail on the driver's side. My precious car scraped along the length of the guardrail as it grounded to a halt. The event was played out like a slow motion sequence in a movie. But at least I was alright, or so I thought.

Anyone who has ever been in a life-threatening situation tells you that time does funny things. Ten seconds seems like forever. After the car had stopped, I took a moment to take a quick inventory.

Did this really just happen? Apparently so.

Am I still alive? As far as I could tell.

Was the car okay? Not that okay.

Anything broken?

"BANG!"

My inventory was interrupted by the loudest sound I had ever heard. After coming to a safe (albeit undignified) stop, the airbag decided to go off. Getting a face full of airbag is a most unpleasant event, I can tell you. "Violent" is the word I would use to describe it. I don't know what condition I was in before the airbag went off, but whatever the condition was, I was definitely in a worse condition now. I always thought an airbag was a big fluffy pillow. How could a big fluffy pillow go "BANG!"?

97

Time began playing tricks again. Somewhere along the way, the airbag deflated. This took either two seconds or 10 hours, I really don't remember. Everything seemed to be happening in slow motion. After awhile (I have no idea of the time frame), I heard a voice through the window. A Good Samaritan had pulled over to offer assistance.

"You should know your arm is broken. The bone is sticking out. Don't move if you can avoid it."

I hadn't felt any pain, so this came as news to me. I didn't dare look at my arm, for I knew that if I did, I would instinctively try to straighten it. About this time, I caught a glimpse of myself in the visor mirror. It was not a pretty sight: my face was all bloody and bruised. I was definitely not having the best of days, and it wasn't even noon yet.

Shortly afterwards, the paramedics arrived. I remembered my car had a sensor that triggers an alert in an accident, and I was impressed how efficiently it worked. My door was jammed against the guardrail, and the paramedics wanted to help me from the car through the passenger door, but, stubborn as always, I insisted on doing it myself. I don't know how I managed it, but I gingerly wriggled myself to the passenger side (after they had checked that my neck wasn't broken, of course). As they were putting me on a stretcher, I started directing people to "call my school, take my handbag – my phone is in there – and DO NOT FORGET MY VIOLIN".

"It's on the back seat. It needs to go with me to the hospital," I insisted. They wisely decided that it was best to do as I said.

I was taken to a small hospital in Orangeburg, where I was given a mountain of forms to fill in. Even in tiptop condition, form-filling has never been my forte. Thankfully, my friends Jerry Dell and Benjamin were by my side – they had rushed to the hospital from Columbia as soon as I called. Jerry Dell and Benjamin were the first to see me in my bloodied state and they were worried sick. After examining me, the doctor decided to transfer me back to the Medical University of South Carolina (MUSC) in Charleston. Given my profession and the nature of my injuries, this was my best bet for getting proper care.

They tried to get a helicopter, but the weather was not cooperating and it wasn't considered safe. So I made the trip back to Charleston on the same road I had just travelled, feeling every bump and pothole along the way. By now, I was starting to hurt more than a little. Since I might have to have surgery at any time, I wasn't allowed pain medication or even a sip of water. As rides go, it was one of the most unpleasant I have ever had to endure.

Time began playing tricks again.

The return trip seemed to take forever, but I don't remember much of it now. When I arrived at MUSC, there was yet more waiting, more form filling; and still no pain medication or water. The first doctor to examine me talked on his cell phone the whole time he was poking me around with a pair of scissors to cut through the bandages around my arm, which by now, was soaked through with blood.

"Hello, can you put that down for just a minute?" I was not a very agreeable customer at that point.

By now, my college had heard about my accident. People started to call. I explained to the secretary that I would not be able to report for the next couple of days, and for her to let ASTA know that I couldn't make it.

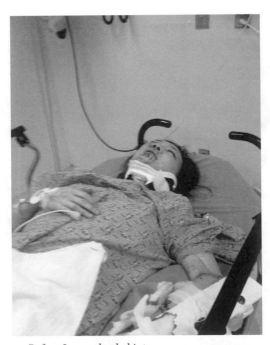

Before I was wheeled into emergency surgery.

"Don't worry about a thing," she soothed.

After what seemed like years, the surgeon finally arrived. Even in my addled state, I was appreciative that I had at least been sent a good-looking one. Besides his good looks, I also noticed how young he was. I suppose after a certain age, everyone else looks young. I just didn't fancy being operated on by a high school student, no matter how good-looking he was. The surgeon introduced himself and we began discussing my injuries and subsequent treatments. Both bones in my lower left arm were broken, but the good news (*good* news!) was that there was no obvious nerve damage.

Then, as is my way, I grilled him: "What is your training, and exactly how many of these things have you done?" It turned out his specialty was sports injuries, not exactly a musician's specialist, but a pretty good substitute.

100

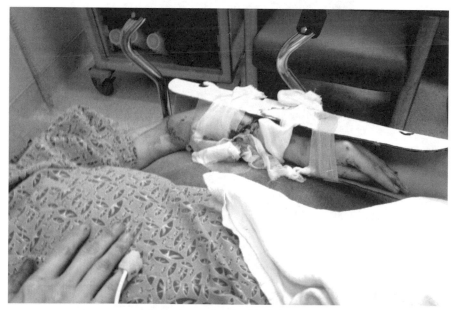

A close-up of my broken left arm.

In a perfect world, I would go to New York and see some top specialist, but that wasn't going to happen. There just wasn't enough time. I wanted the surgeon to know there was a great deal riding on the surgery, so I had the nurses in the exam room show him my website. I was a concert violinist and my livelihood depended on it.

He assured me that he had done hundreds of similar cases, and was confident he could mend me. "Make me as good as new," I think that was what he said. So I agreed that he could operate on me. Some 12 hours after the accident, I was taken to the Operating Room where I finally got some much-needed sleep.

I awoke the next morning in pain, but it was not as bad as I had expected. Everything had gone well. I was lucky it was a clean break. My arm was set in place with titanium plates and screws and would probably heal well. I resolved there and then to be a good patient and do everything they asked of me. I was just a bit upset that I would have to trade glamorous concert gowns for hospital gowns. Not only were they drab, but also draughty.

I was discharged the next day. Thanks to my colleagues and friends, who flooded me with bouquets, my house looked like a flower shop. The well-wishes may have boosted my spirits, but I knew there was a long healing process ahead of me. In the beginning, small things that I had taken for granted, like putting on clothes, tying shoelaces, taking a shower and just lifting my arm, were extremely difficult. The hospital had given me strong painkillers, which made me so nauseous that I preferred to bear the pain instead. I stopped the painkillers after several days and discontinued the homecare that the hospital had arranged. I wanted to get back on track myself — immediately.

Flowers from well-wishers

102

Due to my profession, the doctor put me on an aggressive course of physiotherapy sooner than he otherwise would have done. Living up to my competitive streak (ask anyone who's played me at Scrabble), I wanted to be the best patient they had ever known. Within a week of my accident, I started going for physiotherapy. I couldn't drive and had to depend on friends to take me there. Dealing with the psychological part was the toughest. Just getting into a car was scary – I kept getting flashbacks of the accident. The only silver-lining was that I had lost weight without having to resort to exercise!

The road to recovery was long and arduous. To speed things up, I saw two physiotherapists and went for two or three sessions a week. Therapy actually made the pain worse, but I was determined to get through it. I had to work on regaining the strength to execute simple arm movements, which we all take for granted. In addition, being a good violinist had a great deal to do with touch, feel and fine motor control. I was having trouble with all three. My left hand was weak and there was some numbness in my thumb.

There was one blessing though.

It turned out that because I'm so used to holding the violin in position, I had hyper flexible pronation. While all other arm movements were painful for me, I was able to bring my left hand to shoulder height and position my fingers as if I were playing again.

I knew I would eventually have to face the violin again. One day, a friend asked me to take it out of its case and try it. I attempted a simple scale, something even a beginner can do. Every note was shaky. I struggled with intonation and could barely get through an octave. My hands felt wobbly and weak. It was too much.

I burst into tears.

Psychologically, it was a huge setback. For someone who has performed since a child, my violin is my voice, and the thought of not being able to express myself through it was terrifying. Even if I could play again, one of the best parts of my sound, the vibrato, was a product of my left arm.

Would it ever be the same?

Was I ever going to make my violin sing again?

As I struggled through those dark moments, Dad's words came back to me. When I was little and didn't want to practise scales, he had gently chided me, "There is beauty in the mundane."

103

I clung on to those words as I tried to pick myself up. The accident had thrown my life out of sync and practising scales became a symbol of the routine that I was desperate to reclaim. Being a teacher had its blessings. I had always urged my students to keep walking one step at a time, even though they sometimes weren't sure where the path was headed. I realised there was no better time to be an example to them.

Three weeks after the accident, I started teaching again. I couldn't drive to school so my students came to my home. Resuming my routine, working on my sound one note at a time and teaching one lesson at a time, I started to feel normal again.

When students didn't want to practise, I took it as an opportunity to do it with them.

"Let's do scales together," I would say.

I did my exercises and went to therapy, taught and played as well as I was able. Note by note, scale by scale, I worked on putting my life back together again.

But as the old saying goes, "Misfortunes never come alone". In the early summer, I received an urgent phone call from Singapore. Lady McNeice, who was like the grandmother I never had, was critically ill. I was devastated. I put everything aside, applied for leave and took the first flight home, with my titanium-reinforced arm still in a sling. Lady McNeice was one of the dearest people to me. I had known her since I was 15. Through the years, she had done so much for me and my family and never asked for anything in return. She was one of the most generous and genuine people I ever met. My family and I are indebted to her.

When my brother Yew Nam and I visited her at her home in Singapore, she was lying in bed, drifting in and out of consciousness. We talked to her, but she didn't respond. Yew Nam and I had played for her at her 90th birthday, and we had brought our violins along again that day.

Lady McNeice loved music and it was the best way I could express how she meant the world to me. We played the Bach Double Violin Concerto. I wasn't sure if she heard it, but at one point she opened her eyes, and smiled. Beneath the sadness, that fleeting moment gave me comfort.

Sadly, Lady McNeice passed away a few days later. She was 94, and her last moments were as she wished – at home, next to her beloved garden with her loved ones at her side. As a testimony of the many lives she touched and the contributions she made, hundreds, possibly thousands, came to pay their respects. The President of Singapore, Dr Tony Tan, attended the funeral service at St George's Church.

Yew Nam and I played Bach again at the service. Despite our best-laid plans, life seems to have its own path for us.

In my heart, I had many questions.

What is life, with all its twists and turns, trying to teach me? What am I supposed to learn from all this?

I wasn't expecting to play for several months, at least. I had cancelled my concerts for the summer and had intended to make a comeback only in the fall. Thankfully, I had recovered sufficiently to make it back to see Lady McNeice and was able to play for her one last time. She had supported me throughout my studies in America and helped me realise my dream of becoming a musician.

I am comforted that she was the first to hear me play again.

WILD WILD EAST

I love Charleston. It is a beautiful city in the state of South Carolina, on America's southeastern coast; a place where nature and art come together in what I can only describe as a symphony for the senses. I love it for its blend of old-world architecture and new-world cultures, both of which are evident on every street corner. Charleston is home to Spoleto USA, one of North America's biggest arts festivals. During the festival, the city transforms itself into a paradise for artists and art lovers every summer. Charleston is where I have a house (within walking distance of the Atlantic Ocean), a great job and many wonderful friends.

Since I was a teenager, I have spent more of my time living in the US than in any other country in the world. I have moved with ease from Philadelphia, to New York, to Oberlin, to Chicago, and to Charleston. Of course, there were the times when I wished I could be closer to my parents in Singapore. But never in my wildest dreams would I have imagined a move to China.

The years 2011-2012 were a traumatic time for me, and by 2013, I found myself re-evaluating my life and questioning just what it was I wanted and just where it was I was heading to. I felt a strange inner desire to uproot and move to a totally new environment. If I could have had a complete make-over, I would have done that too.

On the professional front, things were going well. I was more than thrilled that my CD *Songs My Father Taught Me*, recorded as a tribute to Dad, had been so well received. One day, I walked into a HMV store in Singapore and was surprised to see it at the top of the classical charts. Besides teaching, I was also kept busy with my performances in the US and Asia, and by January 2011, I had completed a whirlwind tour of Beijing, Shanghai, Hangzhou, Chongqing and Wuhan, which culminated in a sold-out concert at Singapore's Esplanade Concert Hall. In addition to all of this, I was dreaming up ever more new projects, including writing a book.

I spent that summer in Singapore, happy and blissfully unaware what lay around the corner in wait for me. One day, my brother Yew Nam and I were chatting casually while taking the lift down from his apartment. Yew Nam, who as a doctor is all too familiar with my hypochondriac tendencies, usually shies away from making any medical comments or recommendations. Yet, on this occasion (call it Divine intervention), despite the dim lighting in the lift, he commented that my neck looked a little swollen.

"That looks unusually large," he said, pointing to my thyroid. "Has it always been like this?"

I looked in the lift mirror. He was right. It did look a bit large.

Hmmm.

Yew Nam suggested that I should get it looked at before I returned to the US, just for peace of mind. He set up an appointment for me to see a doctor, who did a biopsy on the spot. I am terrified of needles, and was appalled when he poked a needle into my neck without anaesthesia! To my relief, the doctor said he found nothing and declared I was fine. I just had to follow up regularly to check that it didn't develop into anything nasty. I was enormously happy to leave it at that.

A few days later, Yew Nam had lunch with a close friend of his, whose husband, Dr Mark Khoo, was a thyroid specialist. In passing, Yew Nam mentioned my swollen neck, and Mark said, "Why don't you have her come to see me?" So Yew Nam set up an appointment with Mark for a second opinion, just to be sure. I went along with the arrangements, since it was just a precaution to confirm the first doctor's findings... or so I thought. My appointment with Mark was on a Saturday morning. Yew Nam didn't have to work that day, and so he accompanied me.

Mark explained that a negative biopsy didn't rule out malignancy. He ordered an ultrasound right away, and didn't like what he saw. The images looked cancerous. Leaving it alone was not an option. Mark went through all the different scenarios, from best to worst case. When we left his clinic, it was late in the afternoon. I was in a daze and couldn't absorb all that was being thrown at me. What was supposed to have been a routine consultation had turned out to be a traumatic diagnosis. Anyone who has had a brush with the "C" word knows the fear it strikes in your heart. The grim reaper comes close enough to cast a shadow on your path and stop you in your tracks.

Yew Nam took me out to dinner that night. In the shortest time imaginable, my world had been turned upside down, and I was so glad to have my brother there for support and to guide me on the best course of action to take. Since it was just a few days before my flight back to the US, we decided it was best to follow up with surgery there.

Back in Charleston, I consulted friends who were doctors, Googled and researched everything I could find out about thyroid cancer. Apparently, if you had to have cancer, this was a good one to have as it had a high cure rate (as if that was any consolation). My friends recommended me to see Dr Carneiro-Pla at the Medical University of South Carolina, considered one of the best in her field. It was a godsend that she was based in Charleston.

The moment I met her, I felt I was in good hands. She spoke with a reassuring tone as she looked me straight in the eye. She had the equipment to do a combined biopsy with ultrasound so she could see exactly where the troublesome spots were and zoomed in on them. As with Mark, she also didn't like what she saw and it didn't take her long to confirm the results I already feared. She explained the implications patiently. Because the area was so close to my larynx, there was a danger I could lose my voice. She advised surgery right away and we settled on August 29.

The morning I went into surgery I felt strangely calm. Usually, I agonise over tough decisions, but once the course of action is clear, I'll just head straight for it. The surgery took more than three hours, and Dr Carneiro-Pla seemed happy at how it went. She had removed my thyroid and given me an excellent prognosis. I was discharged after a couple of days. Hooray!

While no one wishes to have a major interruption in their life, I was thankful how Yew Nam's chance meeting with Mark saved me and stopped the cancer in its early stages. Had it not been for Mark's spot-on diagnosis, I wouldn't have been so proactive with treatment, since I was under the impression that the nodule was benign. Finding a professional and highly skilled surgeon like Dr Carneiro-Pla was another huge blessing. She gave me the confidence that I could leave things in her hands, while all I had to focus on was getting well.

During the days following surgery, my voice was a little hoarse and a little quiet, but it gradually improved. After a while, I regained much of my volume and – most importantly for a Singaporean – I could eat normally again. Radiation treatment followed a month later, and the experience was not unlike walking into a nuclear reactor. A security guard escorted me to a room where I was given an armour-clad pillbox. I swallowed the innocent-looking pill contained therein. I didn't realise it at the time but that was the easy bit. In fact, the only easy bit. The less easy bit was that the treatment made me emit radiation, so I had to be isolated for almost a week. I shut myself up at home, meals were left at my doorstep, and everything I touched had to be wiped down. Even my favourite dishes tasted metallic. I lost my appetite. It was downright depressing.

Dr Carneiro-Pla was initially worried about scarring, since Asians have a higher tendency to form keloids, but I healed well and the scar is now barely noticeable. I went for a full-body scan a month after radiation treatment and was given the all-clear. All things considered, everything had gone well, but I had grossly underestimated how much the little butterfly-shaped thyroid gland affects your body.

When it's doing its designated job, nobody notices it. But when it's gone, the body's metabolism, energy levels, heart rate, blood pressure, body temperature, skeletal development and weight (this worried me most!) goes haywire. Loss of bone density and its implications was another big worry.

After my thyroid was removed, I was dependent on the drug Synthroid to replace the hormones normally produced by the thyroid gland to regulate the body's metabolism. I have to take Synthroid for the rest of my life. I followed up with an endocrinologist to work out a treatment plan. I had to learn how to manage my hormone levels, have my blood drawn every three months to monitor it, and make sense of the reports when they came back. It took a while to work out the dosage of Synthroid, as it works differently for each patient.

During this period, I experienced several side effects too.

As if I was not already enough of a Type A personality, Synthroid made my heart beat even faster. I also started getting tingly sensations in my fingers because the calcium levels in my blood were affected by a missing hormone, which the thyroid normally produces. I had to have a supply of calcium by my side to curb the tingles when they struck. Faced with a mountain of pills and supplements, there were times when I would mix them up. Once, I mistook a sleeping pill for Synthroid and popped it into my mouth first thing in the morning before breakfast (when I usually take Synthroid). I was knocked out for the rest of the day! Even when I got the medication right, I was constantly tired and my head felt foggy, but I just kept soldiering on because it's the only way I know. I didn't realise that the tiredness and fogginess were all part of the process of recovery and rebalancing, both of which takes time. Unaware that I needed more time to recuperate, I resumed my concert schedule as soon as I could.

In January 2012, barely four months after my surgery, I returned to Singapore to perform with the Singapore Symphony Orchestra (SSO) at its 33rd anniversary concert. Playing at home with family and friends in the audience is always special, but this concert was an especially emotional one for me. Dad had been suffering from Parkinson's disease for several years, and by this time, he had great difficulty walking. Yet, true to form, he insisted on attending my concert and all the rehearsals. It broke my heart to see him struggling just to get into a seat, and it made me even more determined to play my very best.

For Dad and me, this occasion was especially meaningful – it was our reunion with the orchestra we had played in when it was first formed. Many friends with whom I had grown up with are still in the SSO, and making music with them again felt like a homecoming in every sense of the word. In addition, I was playing Saint-Saëns' third violin concerto, the very same piece that my teacher Aaron Rosand had played with the SSO years before when he had recruited me to Curtis. In so many ways, I had come full circle.

The rehearsals couldn't have gone better, and on concert day, the hall was full to overflowing. When I stepped on stage, I was as ready as I ever had been to relish in the moment of music making. The first movement went well. Then somewhere in the second slow movement I was thrown out of sync, and for a few short seconds I had a memory slip with the harmonics that Rosand had me mesmerised with.

I had never, ever made a slip there before.

Momentarily stunned, I took a deep breath and willed myself to keep going. The show had to go on, and I had done this so many times without any problems. There was still a very exciting third movement and I heard Dad's words in my heart, "You can do it. Enjoy the music and the rest will take care of itself." Right there and then, with the entire audience before me and the orchestra behind me, I had to be my own cheerleader. I charged forward, and the third movement went brilliantly.

As performers, we truly are masochists. Even though we put our reputation on the line every time we walk on stage, no one can stop us from performing. While we all strive to play our best, memory slips happen, even to the most famous of professionals.

At a concert in Vienna, someone counted no less than eight memory lapses by the great Russian violinist David Oistrakh when he performed the Beethoven Concerto. But that didn't make him a lesser violinist. The real challenge was, is and always will be in how you pick yourself up again and again. As a musician, you quickly learn how to acquire the mental strength to carry on even when you stumble. Even in front of a hall full of people.

So that was the year I picked myself up from a pretty low place; a year when it seemed as if life was hell bent on testing me to my limits, with challenge after challenge. There was a time in Singapore when success was defined by the acquisition of the infamous five "C"s: cash, car, credit card, condominium and country club; but during this period I found myself focusing on a different category of "C"s altogether.

Just two months after the SSO concert, I met with the second big "C"—the car crash that broke my arm. As I was building myself up again, Lady McNeice passed away, and in the fall, Dad was hospitalised with pneumonia. Half of me was in denial – surely nothing bad could happen to Dad – and the other half of me was focusing on the rebuilding of my arm so that I could make a comeback in Charleston. I was planning a return during the Christmas holidays when Mom called to ask why I wasn't back yet. It was almost too late.

I wasn't prepared for what I was about to see when I arrived at the hospital. Dad was painfully thin. Parkinson's had advanced to a stage where he couldn't swallow. For two months, he had only taken in liquids via a tube. I was distraught when he didn't respond or recognise me. Barely able to hold back my tears, I reached for my violin – the gift that had bonded us over the years – to play his much-loved piece Jeanie with the Light Brown Hair. It was an especially fitting piece because Mom's nickname for me is Jin (Cantonese for "Chin"). It was my way of telling Dad that his little girl had come home.

Within minutes of hearing the music, tears began rolling down his cheeks. He had recognised me. The nurses urged me to continue. It was a positive step since he had been unresponsive for weeks. I continued to play for him and miraculously, within a day or two, he perked up enough for the nurses to restart therapy. For the first time in weeks, he was able to sit upright on a chair, albeit briefly. I became the resident violinist in the ward.

Initially, I was worried the other patients might be disturbed, but music actually helped break the ice. A lady whose husband had been in the ward for several months came over to tell me that they both felt comforted by my playing. As Christmas was around the corner, the nurses also brought cheer by singing carols from ward to ward. The experience reaffirmed my conviction that there is a certain intangible magic about music. This time, it had a way of banishing the gloom of sickness and despair.

One of the days when I was by his side, I decided to play Dad the Mendelssohn Concerto, which he had taught me. At one point, I fumbled with the fingering and mumbled to myself that I should practise. Dad surprised me by saying in Chinese, "Yes, you must practise more." These words will remain engraved in my mind forever. They were Dad's last words to me.

Sadly, his decline was irreversible, and we were grief stricken when he passed away just two days before Christmas. In mourning, I found solace knowing that the gift of music, which Dad had selflessly bequeathed to me by letting me go away, had brought us together again in his last days.

That Christmas was a time of deep reflection. Would every Christmas be so sad? Within six months, I had lost two of the most precious people in my life. First Lady McNeice, and now, Dad. I was diagnosed with cancer, then I met with an accident that had threatened to end my performing career.

Life is precarious, life is short.

Were the heavens trying to tell me something?

When I was in primary school, I had acted in a school play as the Prodigal Son. Had the role come true? Over the years, I felt guilty that I didn't spend enough time with my parents and always remember Dad's words to me when I left for America: "饮水思源" (Remember the source that quenches your thirst). Dad had yearned for me to work closer to home, but there never seemed to be an opportunity. Yet, three months after his passing, out of the blue, I was invited to take on a professorship at a new school of music in Soochow University, China. My college in Charleston was willing to grant me a leave of absence.

After a year roughing it out, physically and emotionally, I took this as a positive omen. Perhaps I needed to do something completely different to break the chain of bad luck. I decided to return to Asia for a new adventure.

There's a famous Chinese saying that celebrates the beauty of Suzhou: "上有天堂，下有苏杭" (Above is heaven, below is Su-Hang.)[18]

Steeped in 2,500 years of history, generations of musicians, poets, painters and calligraphers have immortalised Suzhou's sublime classical gardens, pagodas and arched stone bridges over narrow canals which have charmed travellers all over the world since Marco Polo's visit in 1276.

I found it inspiring to be surrounded by such artistry and refreshing to be reminded of my own Chinese heritage. Dad's side of the family were Hakkas who originally came from Guangdong, China. Through mass migration, the Hakka diaspora is dispersed all over the world, and now my own wanderings had brought me, by a twist of fate, back to China.

By sheer coincidence, I was in a part of Suzhou that Singapore had a stake in building. Twenty years ago, visionaries from Singapore and China came together to build Suzhou Industrial Park (SIP) on the eastern outskirts of Suzhou. The result is a thriving economic zone full of beautiful lakes, green parkland, sweeping boulevards, gleaming skyscrapers, modern residences, concert halls, museums, schools and universities, where once there had been only farmland and fish ponds.

The greenery, in particular, reminded me of Singapore, and made me feel right at home. When I was introduced to the officials and business leaders who created SIP, I was astonished, impressed and thrilled to learn that many of them had an abiding passion and deep knowledge of music and the arts. These visionaries, who had the imagination to dream up a

116

---

18 Hangzhou is another ancient city close to Suzhou. The Chinese believe that the beauty of both cities (Su-Hang) is comparable to heaven.

new city where there was previously nothing, had turned their vision into one of the richest areas in the province, and in thus doing, could claim to be artists in their own right.

As I plunged into my new life in Suzhou, surrounded by its history and impressive grandeur, I was to learn one of the most awesome lessons I had hitherto learnt. I learnt it not from the university, nor as the result of being an artist, but from a five-year-old boy!

Dad had a gift for teaching children, but I always focused on the older ones since I taught at university level. One day, a local violin teacher introduced me to the parents of a five-year-old boy. They lived in Changzhou, a two-hour drive away, and had heard that I was teaching at Soochow University. Such was their enthusiasm – they were quite prepared to travel to Suzhou every week just so their son could take lessons with me privately.

The boy's name was Xing Xing, and he was practically a beginner. I wasn't overly keen to teach a beginner, but I didn't know how to tell the parents this. In Chinese culture, it is impolite to reject someone with an outright "No", and being used to a more direct and open culture in America, I had to think carefully how to turn them down gently, without causing offence.

In the end, I decided to set him a test, one that he would surely fail. I chose a piece by Beethoven for him to sight-read on the spot. To my surprise, he played it well, and at the end even exclaimed happily in Chinese, "This is Beethoven's Ode to Joy!" My jaw hit the ground with a thud. He had such an infectious love for music, I just couldn't bring myself to turn him away.

And so, I decided to take him on.

117

As I taught him, I found myself, by degree, getting hooked by the challenge of engaging a little boy who couldn't even sit still. (Having no kids of my own, it took a while before I discovered that stickers were a better carrot than a stick!) He had a book of Chinese folk songs, so we started with those. He read music so well and so quickly that it became exciting for me to watch his progress week by week. In the end, I began looking forward to his lessons with relish.

After the Chinese folk songs, we moved on to simplified Western classical pieces, like The Swan from Saint-Saëns' Carnival of the Animals and jazzy tunes from Gershwin's Porgy and Bess. As he progressed, I

With my student Xing Xing

slipped new technical challenges into each new piece. He loved playing with me, and so every lesson we finished off playing duets. Five months after his first lesson, he performed Bach and a Chinese folk song in his first Christmas concert.

One day, he arrived for his lesson with a present for teacher. Shyly, he handed me a sheet of music – a piece he had composed himself! Could I play it for him? Again, I was awestruck. At five, I had been struggling to strike up a tune on the piano!

Xing Xing opened my eyes to the infinite possibilities of what a child can do when you set high expectations. The trick, I soon realised, was to show kids how cool it is to do something well, rather than to scare them with all the technical stuff. Xing Xing had unknowingly taught me another great lesson in my life, and with it, perhaps another new direction. It's ironic that it took a five-year-old to show me how I could help children through music. It was both humbling and inspiring in equal measure. Could Dad have been guiding me on how I could really make a difference? Was this my future?

The Chinese sage Confucius once said, "To educate somebody, you should start from poems, emphasise on ceremonies, and finish with music." Perhaps Dad had wanted me to travel to my source to realise that the wise men of both East and West treasured the power and possibilities of music. Confucius valued music, as did Plato:

"Music gives a soul to the universe,
wings to the mind,
flight to the imagination
and life to everything."

119

Life is a journey; it most certainly has been for me. It has a beginning, a middle and an end. We grow, learn and mature; we gain wisdom and experience, and most importantly of all, we learn to accept the good with the bad, knowing that either can come along at any time, often when we least expect it. How we deal with these situations defines us; makes us who we are. It's all part of the wonderful trip we call Life.

For me, luck, hard work and good looks could only get me so far. I also needed good people around me to inspire, cajole, and lend a helping hand. Family members, friends, teachers, students. Be they 5 or 90.

Through my experiences, from the humorous to the harrowing, I have learnt that when things fall apart, they will come together again.

I truly have come full circle. And the journey is far from over.

Recital at Suzhou Museum *(Photography by Jase King)*

TAKING IT
ONE NOTE AT A TIME

They say that seven is a lucky number, and true enough, the seven notes of the musical scale can create so much magic – they form the foundation of every piece of music we hear and play.

The scale is my metaphor for the basic principles of life that have guided me on my journey. I have put together these little notes to help you perform your best and create magic in your life!

C Create your own opportunities. Be proactive.

D Do not worry about the harvest. Keep sowing, and the rest will take care of itself. (只顾耕耘，不顾收获)

E Explore new things. Take on challenges that scare you.

F Follow your inner voice. Don't follow the herd.

G Go back to your source. (饮水思源)

A Always be prepared. You never know when Lady Luck will come knocking.

B Beauty is in the mundane. To perform your best, you first need to nail the basics.

ACKNOWLEDGEMENTS

While writing this book, I sought advice from my good friend Graham McEune, author of the highly entertaining travel narrative Upcountry. I love Graham's writings with his trademark dry British wit, and having his thumbs-up after reading my first chapter was a huge boost which kept me going. Whether he was in Singapore, Malaysia, or a village in the depths of rural England, Graham patiently dispensed his editorial suggestions and corrected my grammar. It was a painful revelation to know that I had such terrible tenses! Just as well that I decided to stick with music!

To all my teachers and mentors who made me the person I am today, I owe a huge debt of thanks: Dad, whose teachings continue to guide me; Lady Yuen Peng McNeice for inspiring me with her kindness and generosity; Aaron Rosand, Jascha Brodsky, Felix Galimir and the Vamoses who endowed me with a rich musical tradition that I'm privileged to share with young musicians and audiences around the world.

My mom and brothers Yew Nam and Yew Mun have always been there for me no matter how far I've wandered from home; I thank them from the bottom of my heart. Friends in Singapore, America and China have included me as part of their extended family wherever I am. They have been an integral part of my journey. My thanks to all of them, especially Kevin Bourque and family, Jerry Dell and Benjamin Gimarc, Dr Timothy Lyons, Goh Toh Sim and Woi Lee, Lim King Boon, Calipe Chong and Amy Zhao, Dr Serene Lim, and friends from Raffles Girls' School for their unconditional friendship and support.

I would also like to thank Mr Alan Chan, Chief Executive Officer of Singapore Press Holdings, Ms Susan Long for her valuable editorial insights and her entire team at Straits Times Press for publishing my first book. I am grateful to Jean Tan and Lau Wei Yi, who have been my extra pair of eyes in this project. They have rendered much of their time and help.

Finally, my deepest gratitude and special thanks goes to Mr Chan Ming Keng, Chairman of JingHope Holdings Pte Ltd, for believing in me and for his generous support, which brought this project to fruition.

Sincerely,
Lee Chin